EASTER GRACE

EASTER GRACE

Daily Gospel Reflections

By the Daughters of St. Paul

Edited by Maria Grace Dateno, FSP,
and Marianne Lorraine Trouvé, FSP

BOOKS & MEDIA
Boston

Library of Congress Cataloging-in-Publication Data

Easter grace : daily Gospel reflections / by the Daughters of St. Paul ; edited by Maria Grace Dateno and Marianne Lorraine Trouvé.

p. cm.

ISBN 0-8198-2362-7 (pbk.)

I. Eastertide--Prayers and devotions. 2. Catholic Church--Prayers and devotions. 3. Bible. N.T. Gospels--Devotional literature. I. Dateno, Maria Grace. II. Trouvé, Marianne Lorraine. III. Daughters of St. Paul.

BX2170.E35E28 2011

242'.2--dc22

2010018524

Cover design by Rosana Usselmann

Cover photo by Mary Emmanuel Alves, FSP;
interior photo by Mary Emmanuel Alves, FSP

"P" and PAULINE are registered trademarks of the Daughters of St. Paul.

Published by Pauline Books & Media, 50 Saint Pauls Avenue, Boston, MA 02130-3491

Printed in the U.S.A.

www.pauline.org

Pauline Books & Media is the publishing house of the Daughters of St. Paul, an international congregation of women religious serving the Church with the communications media.

1 2 3 4 5 6 7 8 9   15 14 13 12 11

Contents

∴ ⋯⋯⋯⋯⋯ ∵

How to Use This Book

⁞· · · · · · · · · · · ·⁞

Alleluia! Christ is risen!

Easter is the most important celebration in the life of the Church. It's so important that the Easter season lasts fifty days, and every Sunday of the year is a renewed celebration of the resurrection.

The Gospel readings during the Easter season are taken mainly from the Gospel of John, according to a tradition that goes back to the first centuries of the Church. With this book, you are invited to share with members of the Daughters of St. Paul a prolonged meditation on the deep joy of Easter.

These pages are based on *Lectio Divina* (holy reading), which is a way of praying with Scripture. Our founder, Blessed James Alberione, urged us to nourish ourselves with the Scriptures. He said that when we do this, we "experience interiorly the kindling of a divine fire." Many methods of *Lectio Divina* have developed since the time of early monasticism. Here, the sisters use a simple framework that allows the word of God to make room in our minds and hearts.

The first step, *Lectio* (reading), is to read the day's Gospel passage from a missal or Bible. Read it a few times slowly, perhaps especially noticing the phrase or verse that is listed under the *Meditatio* section.

Next, the *Meditatio* (meditation) expands the meaning of this phrase and explores what it is saying to us today—what God is asking of us, or challenging us to, or offering to us. After reading the meditation, take as much time as you like to reflect on it.

The *Oratio* (prayer) can help you talk to God about what has arisen in your heart, so that the time of prayer becomes a conversation, not just a time to think. God has spoken in the Scripture. We hear the invitation in our meditation, but now a response is called for. Our response is not just to say, "Yes, I want to do as you are asking me," but also to declare, "Help me do it, Lord!"

The short phrase under *Contemplatio* (contemplation) is a way of extending this time of prayer into life. You can silently repeat it throughout the day to help deepen the intimacy with the Lord that you experienced in prayer.

Alleluia! Christ is risen! He is risen indeed!

Liturgical Calendar

Note to the reader: The Easter season encompasses the seven weeks from Easter Sunday to Pentecost. Meditations for the Easter Triduum can be found in *Lenten Grace*.

Most dioceses celebrate the feast of the Ascension of the Lord in place of the Seventh Sunday of Easter. In some places it is still celebrated forty days after Easter, on the Thursday of the sixth week after Easter. Meditations are provided for both situations.

The Sunday readings follow a three-year cycle (A, B, or C) as indicated in the following chart:

Year	Cycle
2011	Cycle A
2012	Cycle B
2013	Cycle C
2014	Cycle A
2015	Cycle B
2016	Cycle C
2017	Cycle A
2018	Cycle B
2019	Cycle C
2020	Cycle A
2021	Cycle B
2022	Cycle C

As the Gospels

were written,

so we read them—

in the light of the

Easter candle.

Easter Sunday

∴ · · · · · · · · · · · · ∴

Lectio

John 20:1–9

Meditatio

". . . she ran . . ."

Mary Magdalene hastens to the tomb in the darkness before dawn. She cannot remain alone; she cannot hold back her longing to be near her beloved; she cannot wait for dawn. Mary is the model for all of us who must rouse our love in the sleepy hours of the night, when we feel cold, alone, perhaps abandoned by God, who seems to have failed us and all our dreams. She leads us by the hand, urging us to rouse our love and seek for God when he seems to have died and left us behind.

This Gospel passage is full of love's running haste. Mary runs to Peter and John, fearing that after Jesus' death she may have lost his body also, the last remaining physical connection to him. Peter and John run to the tomb.

What is Peter thinking? Is he pondering the burden of leadership now that Jesus has died, wondering how to handle it? Or does he faintly hope that his Master, who had claimed he was God's Son, will surprise them in a wonderful way?

John runs faster. Is it only because he is younger? Or does he—the disciple whom Jesus loved, the only apostle who kept vigil on Calvary as Jesus hung dying on the cross—does he keep love burning in his heart? Does he hold onto a love that can see beyond the dark days and hope in God's power to raise from the dead? John is the first one who sees the burial cloths and believes.

Mary, Peter, and John teach us to run in hope, in love, and in belief. We need to run first, even in the dark, to search for the Lord, to commit our hearts to love, and then we will witness the Living Christ in our midst. The resurrection means that Jesus lives—here, now, forever—and has taken us to live as his brothers and sisters, sons and daughters of the Father, for all eternity.

Oratio

Lord, my Love, may I seek you in haste in the darkest days of my life. May my heart thrill at the empty tombs in my life where I discover the power of your strength and see the weight of your glory. O Risen One, may I know you alive in my life, in the world, in the Church, in the Eucharist, at the right hand of the Father. Amen.

Contemplatio

I will awake the dawn.

Monday of the Octave of Easter

∴· · · · · · · · · · · ·∴

Lectio

Matthew 28:8–15

Meditatio

"Say, 'his disciples came by night and stole him.'"

The religious authorities didn't know what to make of Jesus' disappearance, and wanted to squelch any rumors at the outset. So they came up with a tale about theft. People would buy it, they thought.

And people *did* buy it. The story was still circulating when Matthew's Gospel reached its final edit, several decades later. A deep gulf had been dredged between people who passionately believed in the resurrection of Jesus and others who emphatically did not. Our world today is both similar to that world and different from it. The gulf is present, but seldom mentioned. There is little evidence of passionate belief.

Why does the somber season of Lent come so naturally, while the joyous season of Easter seems so challenging? By way of an answer, how often do we think of Easter, once the feast itself has passed?

In some cultures, people used to (and may still do) greet one another during the Easter season with these words:

"Christ has risen!"

"He has risen indeed!"

This beautiful greeting was a reminder of the great mystery they had just celebrated. We can carry these words in our hearts and, after greeting others in our usual way, repeat them in the depths of our soul. May they echo within us throughout the day! In remembering and reflecting on the overwhelming love that God has shown us through Jesus' death and resurrection, we can become—as Saint Augustine expressed it—*alleluias from head to foot.*

Christ has risen—he has risen indeed!

Oratio

Lord Jesus, I believe! But rekindle my enthusiasm. Don't let the skepticism of our secular culture cloud my belief or dampen my joy. You are the Faithful One, living and true. You are the Way, the Truth, and the Life. You are the Resurrection and the Life. You are the Savior of the world. Increase my Easter joy. Let the overwhelming reality of your resurrection illumine my path, guiding me through the obscurity of earthly life to the brightness of eternity.

Contemplatio

I want to *really live* this Easter season!

Tuesday of the Octave of Easter

∴∴∴∴∴∴∴

Lectio

John 20:11–18

Meditatio

"Why are you weeping?"

What a strange question to ask a grieving woman, and from an angel at that! "Why are you weeping?" We find Mary Magdalene at the tomb of her Lord, her Jesus, and we hear God's messenger ask her the reason for her tears and, more possibly, her sobs.

"Where is my Lord?" she pleads. "If you have taken his body, let me know where it is and I will take him away." She is so distressed that she doesn't seem to notice to whom she is speaking. Then the gardener asks her the same question, "Why are you weeping? Who are you looking for?" Mary is becoming upset, worn out by the frenzy and grief. Again she blurts out that she can't find the Lord. "Where have you put him?" The gardener is looking at her. Is it quizzically or compassionately? "Mary," he says, not only to identify himself, but also to help her to identify herself. He could have said, "Why are you crying, Mary? Is it only from grief, or also for joy; joy that the promise has really come true? You have heard me promise many times that I am the Resurrection and the

Life (Jn 11:25). You and the other women have often professed your belief in the resurrection. And now, here I am before you. Do not weep. Do not cling to me. Go quickly to my brothers and assure them of what you have seen." Jesus wants Mary to recognize her own faith, to hold fast to his teaching and, as the first apostle of the resurrection, to proclaim his triumph. Let us all become Easter Marys.

Oratio

Jesus, Lord of life, wrap all our tears and fears in your great promise. We believe you rose from the grave, that you overcame all the suffering laid on you as God and man. Your body was crushed, and your spirit was stifled by the sins and sorrows of humanity. But the response you want from us, as from Mary, is not weeping, but great joy. With her make us witnesses, not of a far-off tomorrow, but of the today of salvation. We adore you, O Christ, and we proclaim you because you are the Savior of the world!

Contemplatio

"I have seen the Lord!"

Wednesday of the Octave of Easter

❖ · · · · · · · · · · · · ❖

Lectio

Luke 24:13–35

Meditatio

> *". . . Jesus himself drew near and walked with them."*

It's easy to imagine those two disciples, grieving and confused, leaving Jerusalem because of their sorrowful disillusionment over Jesus' crucifixion. Discussing and debating, they are caught up in their own conversation, no doubt reinforcing their disappointment. Nothing remains of the high hopes they had placed in Jesus. Although their whole conversation centers on Jesus, they don't recognize him when he walks right up to them.

Instead they stop, as if exasperated and ready to give up. They have had it with hope, promises, and dreams. Discontentment is contagious, and quickly clouds our vision. The two disciples impress on Jesus their disappointment, coming to a halt in their walk as if to emphasize that their dreams have died. Unbidden and uninvited, Jesus takes the initiative and draws near to them. Perhaps he discreetly places himself between the two, respectfully interrupting the cycle of disillusionment.

The text doesn't reveal when they start walking again. But after listening to the disciples' sorrow and disappointment,

Jesus takes the lead in the conversation, and probably in the walk as well. He's not about to leave them where they are, at a dead end. Nor does he allow us to give up hope, if we let him take the lead in our lives. "Beginning with Moses and all the prophets," Jesus explains the Scriptures to them. He recounts for them salvation history, so familiar and yet strangely new, winning their full attention. It somehow seems right to let Jesus take the lead, set the pace, and direct their journey. The disciples follow him to Emmaus, are moved to insist that he remain with them, and receive in exchange the fullness of joy: "their eyes were opened and they recognized him." How often does it happen that we too have the Lord right with us, but we fail to recognize him? As Christians, we walk by faith, not by sight. Let us entrust ourselves to the Lord, even when we do not see him by our side.

Oratio

Lord, through Baptism you dwell in each Christian, but how often I fail to recognize you! You dwell also in me through my baptism, and yet many times I go through the day unaware of your presence. Help me see more often with the eyes of faith, Lord. Help me see you in the people in my life and help me be aware of your sacred presence within me.

Contemplatio

Stay with me, Lord, and let me stay with you.

Thursday of the Octave of Easter

:•············•:

Lectio

> Luke 24:35–48

Meditatio

> *". . . still incredulous for joy."*

Have you ever been "incredulous for joy"? Perhaps you received some good news—an invitation to a wonderful event, or a gift, or an award that you never imagined receiving. At first it seems too amazing, and you search for other possibilities. Is it a joke or a dream? What conditions are attached?

The disciples in the upper room are incredulous for joy (after getting over their terror at seeing what they think is a ghost). They look more closely at Jesus, touch him, and realize that he is not a spirit. But they still can't get over it. They still don't believe that they're seeing Jesus raised from the dead. There has to be another explanation. It is just too amazing.

But Jesus has important things to say to them. He doesn't want them to be distracted, still puzzling over how it could be true. So he asks them a simple, down-to-earth question, something so matter-of-fact that it brings them out of their daze.

"Have you anything here to eat?" They find some leftover fish from dinner and give it to him. They watch as he eats it.

They have eaten with him many times over the past few years. The simple act of eating brings them to accept the truth, and Jesus goes on to speak with them about the Scriptures and how they must be the witnesses for him.

Jesus is alive. It's true! He has conquered death. We are invited to live his life, to be made utterly new. We can't waste time being incredulous. Haven't we been touched by his love in so many ways? Haven't we eaten with him? He has something to say to us. When we stop questioning, we will be able to hear what it is.

Oratio

Jesus, sometimes the new life you offer me seems too good to be true. But I believe in you. I believe that you died and rose again. I believe that you speak to me through your word. Are you asking me to offer the hope of new beginnings to someone who thinks it's too late to start again? Am I being called to witness in some other way? I want to listen carefully, to be open to what you want to say to me, to all the ways you are calling me to witness to you.

Contemplatio

Speak, Lord. Your servant is listening.

Friday of the Octave of Easter

⋮⋅⋅⋅⋅⋅⋅⋅⋅⋅⋅⋅⋅⋅⋅⋅⋅⋮

Lectio

John 21:1–14

Meditatio

> *"I am going fishing."*

Sometimes we don't know what to do next. After follow-ing Jesus for years, we think that we understand how God is at work in our lives. We know exactly where we're going. But as the disciples experienced during Holy Week and Easter, following Jesus sometimes turns our lives upside down. Before, things seemed so predictable; now, we are suddenly plunged into the unknown. In such moments we are left wait-ing for the Lord, like the disciples in the Gospel. He had already appeared to them since his resurrection. But what were they to do next? Like them, we ask: how do we spend this time of waiting for the Lord?

In today's Gospel, Peter can't sit still any longer. He doesn't know what to do next, but he has to do something. So he does what comes so naturally to him: he goes fishing. In this darkest hour of his life, this impetuous fisherman returns to the sea. Peter's restlessness touches our hearts. For all its unpredictability, the sea is where Peter most feels at home. At least here, in his fishing boat, he knows what to do. . . . But all through the night he hauls up only empty nets. We can only imagine the frustration he and the other apostles must have felt. Even here at sea, the world no longer makes sense. . . .

But in returning to the sea, Peter is also returning to the place where he first met Jesus. And it is here that Jesus surprises him. In a way that beautifully parallels Peter's first call, Jesus appears and renders their hours of useless toil abundantly, miraculously fruitful. The nets strain to the breaking point with fish. Jesus reassures his closest followers that, no matter what happens, he is always with them. Even as Peter jumps into the water and swims to shore, he may not fully understand where discipleship will take him. But as he recognizes Jesus standing on the beach, one thing becomes clear: Peter will follow Jesus wherever he might lead. And this is the new certainty by which he will live his life.

Oratio

Lord, when I am waiting for you and don't know what to do next, come and call me to yourself again. Bring me back to the moment in which I first heard your voice and let me hear you, calling me anew. Surprise me with your presence in my life and let me recognize your face.

Contemplatio

"It is the Lord!"

Saturday of the Octave of Easter

⁘ · · · · · · · · · · · · ⁙

Lectio

Mark 16:9–15

Meditatio

> *"When they heard that he was alive and had been seen by her,*
> *they did not believe."*

Imagine being in the upper room. Apostles and disciples, men and women, are gathered for safety. The disciples are close to despair, hovering on the edge of hope. Their dreams have been shattered. They had asked Jesus what they would receive if they followed him—and he had promised them so much! Now he was dead. His life ended ignobly—or so it seemed. Someone in the group reminds them that Jesus had said he was the Way, the Truth, and the Life. If he was the Life, the speaker wonders, then how do we understand his death?

Suddenly Mary Magdalene bangs on the locked door. They all look at each other, afraid to open it. Mary continues knocking. The door finally opens and Mary bursts into the dark room with her message, light streaming into each darkened corner: "He is alive! He is alive! I saw him! I spoke with him!" Mary goes to each person in the room with the message: "Don't fear; he sent me to tell you he is raised!"

When Jesus knocks on the door of our heart, are we afraid to open it? What is our fear? Like the disciples, we may find it easier to ignore the knock, to turn on the television, go shopping, surf the Internet, or turn to another diversion. The light of God shines so brightly, and the news of the resurrection so overwhelms us, that we may have a hard time believing, as did the apostles.

Later, Jesus appears in the same room and chides the disciples for their unwillingness to believe. His reproach is like that of a lover who sends a letter only to later find it unopened. Like Mary we receive a love letter from God. We carry the message to everyone we meet: "Do not be afraid. God is with us! He is alive! He sent me to tell you."

Oratio

Jesus, I renew my baptismal dialogue with you. To your "Do you believe?" I respond, "I do believe!" I pray that this will be a decisive renewal in faith. Transform me in your love, and lead me to a life of communion with my brothers and sisters. I want to bring the message of your love to everyone I meet.

Contemplatio

I do believe, not as an idea, but as fullness of life.

Sunday of the Second Week of Easter — Years A, B, and C

:⋯⋯⋯⋯:

Lectio

John 20:19–31

Meditatio

> *"In the evening of that first day of the week . . ."*

The disciples cower in fear behind locked doors. Mary Magdalene has already brought them astounding news. Peter and John had already rushed to the empty tomb. The word is out that something extraordinary is happening. But fear still rules the hearts of the disciples, who retreat into the shadows behind barred doors.

The Risen One comes into this darkness. His greeting echoes the words that God uttered at the dawn of Creation, "Let there be light. . . ." (Gn 1:3). In the upper room Jesus tells his disciples, "Peace be with you."

John's Gospel reminds us several times in the twentieth chapter that these events happen on Sunday, "the first day of the week." At the resurrection, God hits the reset button. This is the first day of a new creation. Life is reclaimed from the jaws of death and restored to its rightful state: at peace with God, at peace with all creation. On this new day creation awakens to a fresh beginning.

Isn't that what mercy is all about? We want a clean slate and a chance to start over. We ask for healing and mercy for ourselves and for the people we hold dear. Jesus walks into the locked doors and hidden places of our life, and breathes his new life into us.

On that Resurrection first-day-of-the-week, God gives us a new start. It is an ongoing event that we celebrate—and in some mysterious way become present to—each time we participate in the eucharistic liturgy. At Mass we encounter the living, resurrected Jesus. We are privileged to touch and be touched by the Risen One. Refreshed, we start anew.

Oratio

Jesus, God's Mercy Incarnate, give me a greater sense of your mercy working in and through my life. I want to enter into your love and compassion for the whole world. Your incredible gift of a new beginning is meant to be lived, celebrated, and shared with others. Help me to hallow the first day of the week of your resurrection by living Sunday not so much as the week's-end afterthought, but as the starting point of my day-to-day life. Let your mercy be my foundation. In the evening of my days may I hear your greeting of "peace" and welcome.

Contemplatio

It is a new day; a fresh beginning.

Monday of the Second Week of Easter

∴ · · · · · · · · · · · · ∴

Lectio

John 3:1–8

Meditatio

> *"He came to Jesus at night."*

Nicodemus was an honest and sincere man who searched for the truth. He had a certain drive within him. He didn't let his hunger for truth fall by the wayside, nor did he forget about it because it seemed too difficult to understand. Instead he searched for Jesus at night. Why at night? Doesn't this seem like an odd time? Perhaps Nicodemus, a Pharisee, didn't want to be seen publicly with Jesus, lest it appear he was a disciple. Hostility to Jesus was growing. In John's Gospel, night can symbolize the darkness of unbelief. In this scene, Jesus, the Light of the world, gently draws Nicodemus into the light of faith. Nicodemus has gone to see this special rabbi whom he admires but whose teachings leave him perplexed. He wants to sit with Jesus and ask all his questions.

And Jesus listens with love and patience. Nicodemus feels at ease and asks questions that might even appear foolish: "How can a man once grown old be born again? Surely he cannot reenter his mother's womb and be born again, can he?" With what transparency and trust he pours out his soul to Jesus! And Jesus' response is thought provoking: "What is born of flesh is flesh and what is born of spirit is spirit." Jesus is comfortable and honest with Nicodemus. It is a true encounter of love.

What about the uncertainty, frustrations, and problems I face? Do I bring these to Jesus and trust that he will untangle the knots in my daily life? Jesus wants to restore calm and peace to my life and lead me to the truth. Maybe I need to find time in my day to be alone with him. It doesn't have to be a special place or hour but simply a quiet, calm, and trusting space. Nicodemus found his in the darkness of night. And the darkness brought forth light.

Oratio

Lord, so often I become overwhelmed by the busyness of my day. I run here and there, making myself available for the needs at home or at work, and at the end of the day I feel exhausted. I try to forget the problems, fall asleep, and take up the same routine the next day. Help me find what is most important in my life. Inspire me to find time alone with you, so that like Nicodemus I may remain in your presence and learn from you the true meaning of life.

Contemplatio

In the peace and quiet even of darkness, true light awaits us.

Tuesday of the Second Week of Easter

:⋯⋯⋯⋯:

Lectio

John 3:7b–15

Meditatio

"You must be born from above."

Jesus spoke these words in the night to one man, Nicodemus. The Apostle Paul proclaimed and explained them to each and every Christian—to you and me. Hear these words as if spoken to you: "If then you [name] were raised with Christ, seek what is above, where Christ is seated at the right hand of God. [name] Think of what is above, not of what is on earth. For you [name] have died, and your life is hidden with Christ in God" (Col 3:1–3).

Can you trace the story of your rebirth throughout your life? After being reborn in baptism—where I died to sin and rose with Christ in God—I had my first major "rebirth" at the age of twenty-one when I had a stroke. It completely altered my life, and my struggle with the resulting physical and psychological complications have made me who I am today. I had another moment of rebirth during a year of failure. Everything I did turned to dust in my hands or was blocked by someone else. Although it seemed so senseless, I knew deep down that this was exactly the way it was supposed to be. I needed to be undone if I was eventually to look for the things that were above. A third moment of rebirth came when I fell and shattered my arm at age forty-six. I had given my life over to God and asked him to accomplish in me himself all that he desired of me. He took me at my word. Temptations and weaknesses I had struggled with for many years were eliminated in an instant as I had to give up efficiency and be tutored in love and abandonment.

Rebirthing events teach us three things: a new perspective; the power of God's love and grace to change our lives; authentic redirection in every level of our being, something we could never accomplish on our goodwill alone.

Have you traced the story of your own rebirth?

Oratio

Jesus, some aspects of my thinking, behaving, and loving bother me. They are not "reborn from above." No matter how hard I try, I seem unable to change them. Send into my life your gentle yet mighty Spirit to raise me up with you. Accomplish in me yourself all that you desire of me. Amen.

Contemplatio

My life is hidden with Christ now.

Wednesday of the Second Week of Easter

⁂ · · · · · · · · · · · · ⁑

Lectio

John 3:16–21

Meditatio

"God so loved the world that he gave his only-begotten Son . . ."

A true gift is given out of love with no strings attached. The receiver may either accept it with joy, hugging or kissing the giver, or disregard its value and reject it, perhaps ignoring the giver. Jesus compares himself to a gift given to humanity by his Father, who gives us his only-begotten Son so that we may have eternal life through him. The Father offers us his unconditional love. As a loving Father, he only wants the best for us, and he offers this great gift to all. Will we accept this offer and open our hearts to his love? Or will we refuse to accept him and turn away from his love? Will we live in the light or walk in darkness?

Jesus is the light of the world. It is easier and safer to travel during the day than at night, because street signs and landmarks are visible. But at night, even where there are streetlights, it's easier to make a wrong turn or miss an exit on the highway. Dangers may lurk on lonely roads. In a similar way, we can live in spiritual light or spiritual darkness. If we choose darkness, we will see neither our slavery to sin nor our need for God's merciful love. Or we can choose to travel on the path illumined by Christ, the Light of Life. We can choose light over darkness, life over death. We believe in Jesus because we see him as the Truth. We can accept his love and live in the truth, the truth that makes us free. By loving Jesus in return we live the truth. The more we live in Christ, the Light, the more our works "may be clearly seen as done in God."

Oratio

Jesus, my risen Savior, I thank you for proving your love by giving your life for me through your passion and death. I praise you for raising me up to new life, and giving me the promise of living eternally with you, through your resurrection. In the sacraments you continually give of yourself so that I may have the wisdom, strength, and desire to love you in return by offering my life for others. May I never reject your gift of love but always keep my heart open, so that your light may shine through me and my "works may be clearly seen as done in God."

Contemplatio

"Whoever lives the truth comes to the light . . ."

Thursday of the Second Week of Easter

⋮···········⋮

Lectio

John 3:31–36

Meditatio

> *". . . The one whom God sent . . ."*

I can hear in this passage the response to a genuine, profound human need—that of knowing who can be believed. So many television shows are based on this premise. With such a plethora of mystery and courtroom dramas on television, it's hard to believe that new programs based on the same basic plots can make it. Yet they do. What's even more fascinating is that they hold our attention. Why? Because of this deep need—perhaps obsession—to know who is telling the truth. Whose testimony is true?

That is what's happening in this passage from John. It seems to form the conclusion to a disagreement between John the Baptist's "camp" and "a Jew" regarding ceremonial washing. John realizes that the Person of Jesus is at the heart of the disagreement. What he hears in the disagreement is an underlying need to know if Jesus can be believed—is he telling the truth?

Through the gift of the Spirit, it has been revealed to John that Jesus has been sent by God. Unlike others, he alone can communicate about God from what he "has seen and heard." John is a model of one who has received the gift of the Spirit, which is not rationed. He communicates the truth about Jesus, who has been sent from above and is, therefore, able to reveal the intimate relationship shared with his Father. By accepting the revelation of the Spirit, John "certifies that God is trustworthy." By this faith, John stakes his life on this truth to the point of dying to defend it.

Have I accepted Jesus' testimony? Today's Gospel seems to say that this is the key to the discipleship that John models and in which I can participate. I too can be sent by God and speak his words. But that depends on my acceptance of Jesus' testimony, which leads to a certification that "God is trustworthy."

Oratio

Father, you are the One who sent your son, Jesus, into our world. We have just celebrated Easter and commemorated the greatest testimony you gave to your Son—his resurrection. Like the apostles, I don't understand everything you have revealed. Pour out the gift of the Spirit upon me as you have promised—without ration. Thus may I begin to testify to you by my life that I am your Son's disciple. Amen.

Contemplatio

"He does not ration his gift of the Spirit."

Friday of the Second Week of Easter

:⋯⋯⋯:

Lectio

John 6:1–15

Meditatio

"[Jesus] said to Philip, 'Where can we buy enough food for them to eat?'
He said this to test him."

Today we start reading chapter 6 of Saint John's Gospel, which is about Jesus, the Bread of Life. John begins it with the scene of Jesus miraculously feeding the crowd. Even though Jesus knows what he was going to do, he tests Philip by asking him where they can buy enough food for the great crowd. Why does Jesus test him? It could be because John is presenting Jesus in a way similar to Moses. For example, Jesus goes up the mountain like Moses, and Jesus' walking on the water (tomorrow's Gospel) recalls the miraculous escape through the Red Sea. When Moses led the people through the desert, God sent them the gift of manna. But he placed conditions on it: "Thus will I test them, to see whether they follow my instructions or not" (Ex 16:4). In a similar way, Jesus is testing Philip's faith. Philip seems to fail the test, though, because he can't see beyond the bread to what Jesus is really asking. Despite this, the ever-patient Jesus feeds the crowd by miraculously multiplying the loaves and fish.

Jesus feeds us too, not with ordinary food but with his Body and Blood in the Eucharist. We don't have to *buy* this food because he freely gives it to us. "You who have no money, come, receive grain and eat; come, without paying and without cost, drink wine and milk" (Is 55:1). Though freely given, the gift of God's food still requires something of us: the test of faith. Through faith, we can see that Jesus' gift of bread and fish points to his greater gift of the Eucharist. This Gospel is a test for us, too: what do we most value in life?

Enthusiasm sweeps through the crowd for Jesus, the miracle worker who could supply free food. But those in the crowd don't grasp the deeper reality of Jesus. He will unfold it for them through his teaching, but they will end up rejecting him. What about us? Every day, the Church offers us free food at Mass: Jesus himself, his Body and Blood. Are we eager to receive it? Will we pass the test of faith?

Oratio

Lord Jesus, you are the Bread of Life, the Bread that sustains us on our spiritual journey. I thank you for giving us your Body and Blood in the Eucharist. Help me to always receive this sacrament with great faith and trust in you. Transform me day by day into an image of you, so that I may reflect your love to all I meet.

Contemplatio

Jesus, I believe in you.

Saturday of the Second Week of Easter

∴ · · · · · · · · · · · · ∴

Lectio

John 6:16–21

Meditatio

> *"It was now dark, and Jesus had not yet come to them."*

It has been quite a day! After teaching on the hillsides for a long time, Jesus fed his hungry listeners by multiplying five barley loaves and two fish. The excited crowd wanted to carry Jesus off to crown him king, but he withdrew to the mountain alone. Knowing they were only seeking signs and wonders, Jesus did not want to encourage a superficial enthusiasm.

While the disciples wait for Jesus, they ponder the day's events. As the sun begins to set, they decide to cross back to Capernaum even though Jesus has not yet rejoined them. A sudden storm springs up on the lake, and the rough winds stir high waves that began breaking over their boat in the darkness. The stormy sea can illustrate a lesson for us.

In John's Gospel, darkness and night often stand for forces opposed to the light and truth of Jesus. These spirits of confusion, doubt, and conflict are present in the turmoil of the night. Only hours earlier, the disciples had experienced Jesus' compassionate presence and his amazing power to feed the crowds. Their faith in Jesus was growing stronger. But now, in his absence, they grow frightened as the storm engulfs them in the dark. "It is I; do not be afraid," Jesus reassures them as he comes toward them on the water.

Perhaps these events can highlight an important truth of the spiritual life. We can savor the God-given moments of clarity, grace, and consolation so they may strengthen, comfort, and encourage us in difficult times. The disciples had just witnessed a miracle of Jesus. They could have let that experience fill them with trust and confidence in God instead of becoming overwhelmed with fright. As Jesus approached them, "the boat *immediately* arrived at the shore to which they were heading." Buoyed with faith, we too can trust that the mere presence of Jesus, who is always with us, will completely overcome any obstacles we may face.

Oratio

Teach me, Jesus, to trust in you even when the seas in my life grow rough and strong winds are blowing. Allow me to recall the gifts of your presence and peace that have strengthened me in the past, and let them help me patiently endure my present difficulties with courage and trust. Help me to seek your face and to recognize your coming, which I may fail to see because of the difficulties of life. Bring me safely to shore when I am threatened by danger or fear. My comfort and my hope are in you!

Contemplatio

"It is I; do not be afraid."

Sunday of the Third Week of Easter — Year A

:⋯⋯⋯⋯:

Lectio

Luke 24:13–35

Meditatio

> *"[Jesus] gave the impression that he was going on farther.*
> *But they urged him, 'Stay with us. . . .'"*

Sometimes, when we need him most, the Lord appears on the road alongside us. His presence is so unexpected that we don't even recognize him at first. But little by little he helps us to understand how he has been at work in our lives. A moment of sadness or confusion is suddenly lightened, and hope glimmers again in our hearts.

This is how we find the two disciples traveling to Emmaus. Sad and confused, they are unexpectedly encouraged by a complete stranger. This stranger helps them reflect on their experiences in light of the Scriptures, and their hearts begin to burn with a strange hope. As they reach their destination, however, their companion acts as if he means to travel on. . . .

This point in the story of Emmaus may very well give us pause. Jesus has walked far along the road with these two disciples. He has explained the Scriptures to them, listened to them in their heartbroken sadness, and given them new hope. After all this, why should he pretend that he wants to continue the journey alone? We, the readers of this story, suspect that Jesus wants nothing more than to break bread with these two disciples. But having once broken in on their conversation as they walked along the road, the Lord now desires to be invited to remain.

How often God works in our lives in just this way: gently guiding, teaching, helping us to see things from a new point of view, but always respecting our freedom. As he waited for the two disciples to invite him to stay for supper, Jesus waits for our invitation, too. Jesus wants to reveal himself to us through his word and through the Eucharist—but he waits for open hearts, he waits for us to welcome him, before overwhelming our lives with his presence.

Oratio

Jesus, let my heart be an open, welcoming space for you. Even when I do not yet recognize you, my friend and Master, come and stay with me and reveal your presence to me, that I may share the joy of your goodness to me with others.

Contemplatio

The Lord has indeed risen!

Sunday of the Third Week of Easter — Year B

:・・・・・・・・・・・・:

Lectio

Luke 24:35–48

Meditatio

> *"Peace be with you . . ."*

Imagine the apostles and disciples gathered in the upper room on Sunday night. In this very room, four days earlier, the apostles had eaten supper with Jesus, the supper that was his last. He told them, "My peace I give you . . ." (Jn 14:27). They feel anything but peaceful now! Jesus had been tortured; he was "crucified, died, and was buried." And now— all these reports that he has been seen, brimming with life.

"Let's try to pray," someone says, "as he taught us." It is the least they can do to try to keep his memory alive. "Our Father," begin one or two voices, "who art in heaven." Others join in, "Hallowed be thy name." At "Thy kingdom come," a new presence is felt in the room. For the eleven it is like that mysterious moment Thursday evening when they had eaten the bread and drunk from the cup: "My body . . . blood . . . peace I give you." It is as if they can even now hear his voice! "Peace be with you." Then they realize: they are, indeed, hearing *his* voice.

"Peace be with you" on the lips of the risen Jesus is the answer to our prayer: "Thy kingdom come." That kingdom is the fullness of peace—not simply absence of conflict, but (in the words of the classic definition) the tranquility of order. Peace is to the universe what health is to the body: order; the way things are supposed to be. Not static, rigid, lifeless, but a condition of life so full it cannot be threatened or undermined by any power in this world. In him of whom the "law, prophets, and psalms" spoke, in his glorified human body, the body born of Mary, the universe is again set in right order—and an even better order than before! God really can "make all things (*all* things!) work together for good" (see Rom 8:28).

Oratio

Jesus, your greeting of peace reminds me of the angels' song at your birth: "Glory to God in the highest and on earth peace" (Lk 2:14). In the manger, too, you could say, "Touch me: my flesh and bones are real: I came to bring you peace." So often I need to hear your voice and accept your gift of peace, and accept the tranquillity of an order centered in you, who have already "conquered the world" (Jn 16:33). You've been through the worst that this world (and the next) can offer, and you come to us to say, "Peace be with you."

Lord, I accept! Establish your kingdom of peace in my mind and heart, especially in that area where I most need peace today. Make me a witness of heavenly peace to the ends of the earth.

Contemplatio

Glory to God in the highest, and peace on earth!

Sunday of the Third Week of Easter — Year C

:⋯⋯⋯⋯:

Lectio

John 21:1–19

Meditatio

"*Cast the net. . . .*"

The boat rocks gently on placid waters that mirror the coloring sky. Vague shapes can be seen in the semidarkness as the fishermen move about swiftly, casting the net. Once the mesh sinks into the water, the sea boils with fish and the net fills quickly. It almost bursts. All this happens because the disciples had obeyed the dim figure standing on the lake-shore.

In his document for the beginning of the third millennium, John Paul II wrote about another marvelous catch—one recounted in the Gospel of Luke. In that document, the Holy Father urged the Church—urged *us*—to "put out into the deep" (see Lk 5:4) and lower our own nets.

The Pope sent out a call to each of us, and that call needn't frighten us. Lowering the nets doesn't have to involve great things. It needn't require much time. Often it just asks a little effort. We don't need to be gifted speakers or have winsome personalities. We simply need to ask the Lord to work through us, and then avoid getting in his way. If we're convinced of Jesus' unconditional love for us and others, we can do it.

Where to begin?

If my time is limited, I can start very simply. Where can I come out of my comfort zone and do an act of kindness? Is there some good deed I've intended to do but haven't gotten around to? When will I schedule it in? If I provide opportunities, the Lord's goodness can reach out through me.

If I have more time, so much the better. Can I join a church or civic volunteer group, for example? Or simply form the habit of visiting the sick to say a good word?

My world teems with possibilities. How will I respond?

Oratio

Lord Jesus, Risen One, may I see the world with new eyes, bathed in the light of your resurrection. Your paschal mystery has brought you among us in a new way, present through the action of your Spirit but invisible to our earthly sight. You call me to be your hands, feet, and voice, so you can reach out to the people of this time and place through me. You want me to help them know about your love and concern for them. Let me know the right moment and help me choose the right words or actions. Enable me to forget myself so that *you* can act. Amen.

Contemplatio

Yes! At the first opportunity I will "cast my net."

Monday of the Third Week of Easter

⁘· · · · · · · · · · · ·⁘

Lectio

John 6:22–29

Meditatio

> "*. . . Rabbi, when did you get here?*"

Have you ever asked someone a question only to receive a reply that just didn't fit? That's what happened to the people questioning Jesus. They asked a straightforward question: "When did you get here?" If I had asked that question, I would have been looking for an answer like "6:00 AM." Wouldn't you?

But Jesus' response? "Amen, amen, I say to you, you are looking for me not because you saw signs but because you ate the loaves and were filled." If I had heard that, I would have scratched my head and thought *"What?"* To a simple question we get a solemn "Amen, amen" response—a response that says, "What I am about to say is so true that I'm willing to swear to its veracity." Translation: Jesus knows why we came here in the first place. We don't really want to know what time he came here. But we would like some more bread.

Jesus continues by encouraging the people to work for food that "endures for eternal life." Then they ask him: "What do we have to do to accomplish God's work?" Jesus again gives an interesting response: believe in God. But that's not doing anything—not accomplishing anything at all! What kind of response is that?

This dialogue mimics our own dialogue with God. Sometimes when I've asked Jesus questions, the answers didn't seem to fit. But then I discovered that, strangely enough, the response satisfied me. However, I can understand that the strange response truly fits my question if only I believe. I have to believe that the Person to whom I have put my question is not only ready to swear to the veracity of the response—but also that that Person is Truth itself.

Oratio

Jesus, I struggle at times with the responses that I receive to questions I ask you and your Father. Sometimes, the responses I receive aren't responses at all, but questions. Other responses just don't fit. Help me to surrender my way of looking at and understanding things. Grant me the Holy Spirit's gift of understanding. Open my heart to your responses. I know that they answer the questions I was really asking in the first place and may not have had the courage to either acknowledge or direct to you. Amen.

Contemplatio

Jesus, I believe that you are the one sent by God.

Tuesday of the Third Week of Easter

•⋯⋯⋯•

Lectio

John 6:30–35

Meditatio

> *". . . whoever comes to me will never hunger . . ."*

With all due respect, I beg to differ.

I completely identify with Saint Augustine, who exclaimed that you had touched him and now he burned for your peace; he had breathed in your fragrance, and now he forever longed for more. It is true that Jesus is the Bread of Life who satisfies our deep hunger for limitless love and everlasting life. I've tasted this. So why does it seem that my hunger never ends?

When I decided to take my baptismal commitment seriously and enter into a living, conscious relationship with Jesus, it was exhilarating at first. Then reality set in. No matter how much I want to follow Christ, I find other things catch my attention, too. Deeper still, my heart and flesh cry out for security and comfort, and I am tempted to seek temporary satisfactions here and there. I settle for short-term solutions to soothe my inner craving. I argue with myself: "No one can really live up to all the demands of the Gospel! You are presumptuous to think that you can be a witness for Jesus Christ."

But in my heart of hearts I listen again to this reading from John, "I am the bread of life; whoever comes to me will never hunger, and whoever believes in me will never thirst." My endless thirst is met by Jesus' endless gift of life—true life. God's fidelity to his covenant of creation and redemption gives all of us our daily sustenance. The strength of the call lies in the one who calls—not in the one who answers. My seemingly bottomless need for reassurance, signs, and consolation is challenged—but always met—by God's infinite gift of his own life shared in Eucharist and daily experiences of grace. God calls me beyond my small self into his infinite generous expanse. My heart is restless until it rests and is nourished in him.

Oratio

Why do you do this to us, O Lord? Why do you put into our hearts a yearning to follow after you and enter into your life? Our hearts ache and ache, and we reach after you, but it is impossible. Even our best efforts to live as you wish us to, and to love as your heart loves, fall short of the mark. Teach me to live with this paradox: to always hunger after you, the only one who can completely satisfy my deepest longings. You are the Bread of Life. Give us this bread always. Amen.

Contemplatio

Give us this day our daily bread.

Wednesday of the Third Week of Easter

❖・・・・・・・・・・・❖

Lectio

John 6:35–40

Meditatio

> *"Whoever comes to me will never hunger,*
> *and whoever believes in me will never thirst."*

For what do you most hunger? The hunger and thirst that Jesus speaks of in today's Gospel are obviously not a physical need for food and drink, but rather a need or desire on the spiritual level. Each of us has this deep desire, a longing for more. Yet how often we try to satisfy this spiritual longing with material things. We convince ourselves that if we only could have more money, or that flashy car, or that dream house, or that newest digital gadget, or get that promotion—then we will be satisfied. But when we attain each goal, we notice that the satisfaction only lasts a short time. Before long, the yearning that we thought was satisfied returns and makes us desire one more thing. Where does this cycle of longing come from?

Today's Gospel opens our eyes to the reality that deep within we are seeking the infinite—that which lasts forever. Much in our society today is focused on self-interest, encouraging us to do everything for our personal gain and satisfaction. But part of us, deep inside, will never be completely satisfied with earthly things.

When Jesus says that anyone who comes to him will never hunger or thirst, he is identifying himself (as the second person of the Trinity) with God, the Infinite One, who satisfies all our longings. We receive Jesus as the Bread of Life in the Eucharist. We receive Jesus' own life, his very person. When we consume the Eucharist, we are being transformed into the mystical body of Christ. When we eat food it becomes part of us, but when we consume the Eucharist we are becoming Jesus. The Eucharist transforms us by strengthening us and conforming our thoughts, words, and actions to those of Jesus. In that process, it satisfies the deepest hungers of our heart.

Oratio

Jesus Master, thank you for the moments when I touch my deepest longing for the eternal. I thank you for the gift of the Eucharist, the Bread of Life, which begins to satisfy this longing. By your grace, may I grow in awareness of the life communicated to me, which transforms my soul and at the same time sows seeds of the resurrection in my body. Jesus, I come to you. I believe in you.

Contemplatio

Come to me.

Thursday of the Third Week of Easter

※ · · · · · · · · · · · ·※

Lectio

John 6:44–51

Meditatio

"I am the bread of life."

Do you want to live forever? How much would you pay for eternal life? I did an Internet search for the words "how to live forever" and got almost 52 million hits! Some people are going to great lengths to try and live forever, from having their dead bodies frozen in liquid nitrogen in hopes of future revival, to developing gene therapy that short-circuits the aging process. Perhaps a better question is: *where* do you want to live forever? Do you want to live forever on an earth filled with suffering and sadness, or do you want eternal life with God in the perfect happiness of heaven?

In today's Gospel, Jesus tells us: "This is the bread that comes down from heaven so that one may eat it and not die. . . . Whoever eats this bread will live forever." Jesus is telling us the secret of eternal life, the secret that so many desperate people are paying huge amounts of money to discover. It's ironic and a little sad to see them go to such extraordinary lengths to get something that Jesus offers us freely. It would be like excavating a field to dig up a treasure that was sitting in plain sight. As Jesus tells us in this Gospel, faith is the key that unlocks the door to this treasure: "Whoever believes has eternal life." It takes faith to believe that the bread Jesus gives us is actually his body, his "Flesh for the life of the world." But when we receive the Eucharist with faith, Jesus gives us a pledge of eternal life. If we want to live forever, we don't need to have our body frozen after death or to undergo gene therapy. We only need to turn to Jesus with faith, eat his Body and drink his Blood, and after death he will meet us with open arms.

Oratio

Thank you, Lord, for giving us yourself in the Eucharist, our pledge of eternal life. I often get caught up in the mundane details of each day and don't think much about eternal life. But as I live in this passing world, help me to keep my final destination in mind: eternal life with you forever in heaven. I believe in your promise. Lord, increase my faith.

Contemplatio

Lord, you have the words of eternal life.

Friday of the Third Week of Easter

∴ · · · · · · · · · · · · ∴

Lectio

John 6:52–59

Meditatio

> *"How can this man give us his Flesh to eat?"*

In truth, we don't understand these words of Jesus any more than did those who heard them from the lips of the Savior himself. Jesus does not offer any explanation to satisfy their curious intellects. He simply calls for their faith. "Unless you eat the Flesh of the Son of Man and drink his Blood, you do not have life within you." Belief is a matter of life and death, not of understanding. His Flesh and Blood are the medicine of immortality.

Such belief keeps us in the place of the creature, the recipient of the Creator's love and the follower of his plan. Why should we believe something so preposterous as these words recorded in the Gospel of John? We are perfectly free to judge from the point of view of our puny intellect that they are nonsense. We are also free to say that though we cannot understand, we will believe, because the word of God can be trusted.

What follows upon belief? In these past weeks we have meditated on the stories of people who encountered the risen

Christ three days after they had laid him to rest on that first Good Friday. Surprise. Awe. Homage. Speechless wonder. Amazement. The words of Thomas, who received a personal appearance to resolve his doubt, capture the sentiments of all the first disciples in a short prayer, "My Lord and my God" (Jn 20:28).

You and I are privileged not just to *see* Jesus risen from the dead, but to *receive* him—body, blood, soul, and divinity—a privilege not even accorded the angels. What homage should be in our hearts as we, the ones for whom Christ died, receive him in the Eucharist, week after week, day after day. . . . It does not matter *how* it happens; it is enough to know *that* it happens.

Oratio

Jesus, I believe in your presence in the Eucharist. I believe that when I receive you I am your whole world and you are mine. For that brief moment there is just you and I. It is the closest of encounters. Around me people are shuffling by, clearing their throats, singing. Filled with your presence, I join the song, rejoicing that you are also *all* for everyone in the Church with me receiving you. In profound reverence I thank you for this gift.

Contemplatio

Jesus, I yearn for you.

Saturday of the Third Week of Easter

.•.............•.

Lectio

John 6:60–69

Meditatio

"Master, to whom shall we go?"

In response to Jesus' question, "Do you also want to leave?" we see Peter respond with his characteristic spontaneity. His answer comes straight from his heart. The disciples are struggling like everyone else to understand and believe in Jesus' teachings. But they have also had a personal experience of Jesus and his action in their lives. They have never known anyone else who so deeply understands and responds to the deepest longings of their hearts. Jesus has made all the difference in the world, and they cannot turn back!

On some days our discipleship costs a little more. Living God's word, following God's way offers us comfort *and* affliction, consolation *and* challenge. We experience the joy of being accepted and loved as we are. Yet we also hear the invitation to that continuous conversion, to keep getting up when we fall down along the way.

Like Peter and the disciples, we know that walking with Jesus is demanding, and we often have to grapple with things beyond our understanding. Faith does not come easily when it asks us to believe in what we cannot see. Hope is often tested to its core in the face of seemingly insurmountable obstacles, when doors slam shut in our faces. Love requires a total gift of our selves again and again.

Others may look at our lives and think we are foolish. We may even wonder at times why we ever chose a way of life that goes so contrary to the way of the world around us. But we also cannot deny that Jesus has come into our lives and made all the difference. He did say that with him we could do everything, and he sent us the Spirit as the proof that he is true to his word. That Spirit, living in us, makes our discipleship possible day after day.

Oratio

Master, I cannot see you, yet I know you are near. I cannot hear your voice, yet I know you speak to me in the silence of my heart and through the events of each day. I often struggle to understand your ways and the meaning of your words, yet I want to believe. Jesus, you are my Master. Your love has broken into my life and forever changed me. Help me to embrace your words with faith, to follow the way of life you have traced out for me, and to unite myself each day more closely to you.

Contemplatio

Master, you alone satisfy the deepest longings of my heart.

Sunday of the Fourth Week of Easter — Year A

:············:

Lectio

John 10:1–10

Meditatio

> *"I am the gate for the sheep."*

Nowadays no one leaves doors unlocked. That is considered much too dangerous and far too inviting of criminals. We are trained never to speak to strangers, never to go with anyone we don't know. Our parents impart these first rules of safety to us from an early age. These two preventives, however, are contrary to the spirit of loving trust a Christian feels by nature. Yet the Lord himself cautions us to beware of thieves and robbers.

We are less wary and less guarded when it comes to the danger we invite into our souls. In fact, it is impossible to walk the ways of the world without bringing home to our minds, our wills, and our hearts some of this danger. These modern thieves and robbers appear so attractive and appealing. They reach out even to what is best in our human nature, and may slowly siphon off some of our fervor, love, and zeal. These are the cultural crooks. We become so accustomed to them that we let our guard down. We wonder: what harm they can do? After all, we reason, this is the world we are living in.

What choice do we have? Just as the sheep had to leave their pen every day and wander among the hills, so we have to live in our world and engage our culture. God wants us to have life and have it in its fullness. God does not ask that we hide from the world around us. Nor does he want us to shun the world. The choice that we do have is to go through the gate, and to check in with the gatekeeper, as the Gospel recommends. In this case, the gatekeeper is a good conscience, kept alert by God's grace. This grace is our gatekeeper. An attentive conscience nourished and protected by grace enables us to come and go in confidence.

Oratio

Jesus, Good Shepherd, you lead and guide me through this life. Every time I am tempted to wander off, you gently bring me back. So many things attract my attention, call for consideration, beckon for just a glance. Help me by your gift of grace to be always attentive and conscientious, ever grateful for our world and its inventions, but always secure in my faith. Thank you, Lord, for your constant, loving care.

Contemplatio

"I came that they might have life and have it to the full."

Sunday of the Fourth Week of Easter — Year B

⁝⋅⋅⋅⋅⋅⋅⋅⋅⋅⋅⋅⋅⁝

Lectio

John 10:11–18

Meditatio

"A good shepherd lays down his life for the sheep."

After showing the film *Gran Torino* to a group of people, I asked them how they would explain it to someone who had never seen it. One man shot up his hand and said without hesitation, "it was about Jesus giving his life for me."

In *Gran Torino*, Walt Kowalski saves his Hmong neighbors, Sue and Thao, from the ongoing threat of gang violence. He confronts the armed gang members, knowing that they will most likely open fire. As he suspects, this confrontation provokes the gang members to shoot the defenseless Kowalski. After I saw the movie, I put myself in Sue and Thao's place as they watched the lifeless body of Kowalski being placed in the ambulance. Not only were they now safe, but they also knew just how much they meant to Kowalski. They were worth so much to him that he had been willing to die for them. While it is true that Kowalski is not Jesus, in a small way stories like this can help us understand what Jesus did for us.

In this passage, Jesus tells us that a good shepherd is willing to lay down his life for his sheep. He emphasizes this by saying that he lays down his life willingly. Jesus knows that in a world in which we daily face the consequences of sin, we are terrorized by what we have experienced and continue to experience. That is why he laid down his life for us—to save us from an eternity of facing those consequences.

Jesus' life and death are God's way of communicating to us how much we mean to him, how much he loves us. Jesus knows us intimately because he too knows what it is like to face the consequences of sin. He knows how terrifying it is. And to save us from that, he laid down his life. He loves us to the point of death.

Oratio

Jesus—*you* died for me. You *died* for me. You died *for me*. This is so overwhelming that I can't sit with it for very long. It makes me uncomfortable. If I allowed this reality to sink in, I would have to give up the shame I feel in the pit of my stomach. I would have to admit that I am truly precious, that my life has inestimable worth, and that I do not need to be afraid of you. You are the only one who truly knows me. I mean so much to you! Help me to know you better. For you are the only one who can save me from what terrorizes me. Amen.

Contemplatio

You loved me. You gave your life for me.

Sunday of the Fourth Week of Easter — Year C

⁝ · · · · · · · · · · · · ⁝

Lectio

John 10:27–30

Meditatio

> *"I know them, and they follow me."*

Being from a society that esteems personal choice, our ears automatically translate these words of Jesus into something like this: Jesus is a shepherd. Shepherds were probably unimportant people sent out to tend to someone's herd of sheep. Some people have decided to follow Jesus and be part of the flock he shepherds. Those who want to follow Jesus the Shepherd listen to his voice and do what he says. Otherwise, people decide for themselves how best they should live their lives.

In realty, shepherding in Israel was an important position, especially for the chief shepherd, a term given to Christ (I Pt 5:4). The flock *belongs* to the shepherd, for the shepherd has paid for it. Its members have not voluntarily blessed the shepherd with their presence in the flock, and therefore could consider themselves free to leave when they tire of the experiment. They are his property. These words grate on our ears, but in reality, it is so. We have been bought and paid for, as Saint Paul says (see I Cor 7:23). We have been purchased by the blood of Christ (Rv 5:9).

John 10:27–30 sets up the responsibilities of the shepherd and the duties of the sheep. The sheep listen and follow. They depend on, abide in, the truth that the shepherd proclaims. Manifesting the truth is the mission and life's work of the Son of God, the chief Shepherd of our souls. The Shepherd, Jesus, for his part binds himself to know each one of us for whom he gave his life; give us eternal life; guarantee that we shall not perish; and never allow anyone or anything to take us out of the hands of him and his Father.

The image of the shepherd and his flock clearly demonstrates to us the change of masters that has occurred—we are no longer slaves to sin and evil, but the property of the Lord of glory. We have been freed in order to be able to love, which is the deepest fruit of truth.

Oratio

Jesus, good and gentle Shepherd, you have freed me from the tyranny of evil through your life, death, and resurrection, and you are bringing me into the kingdom of light and glory. I hear your words. I understand your calls to me. I desire to live differently, more deeply, more lovingly, to love as I have been loved. How could it be that you pledge your life for mine? Today I give you my life in return.

Contemplatio

"The LORD is my shepherd; there is nothing I lack" (Ps 23:1).

Monday of the Fourth Week of Easter

◦ · · · · · · · · · · · · ◦

Lectio

John 10:11–18

Meditatio

> *"I know mine and mine know me."*

Do you ever feel that you want someone to really know you? Does it sometimes seem that events in your life are taking you away from where you really want to be or from the "true you?" Jacob felt like this. Things had gone well in his life, culminating in that one wondrous moment when his father Isaac blessed him. But then his brother Esau threatens to kill him when he finds out that Jacob has stolen his blessing. Jacob runs away, back to the place his grandfather Abraham had left when God called him. Tired and worn out, anxious and uncertain, Jacob stops for the night. As he sleeps, the God of his father reminds him that he is still blessed because God is his companion on the journey (see Gn 28:10–22). Later Jacob becomes a shepherd in the land of his exile. He realizes that God had always been with him as a shepherd, calling his name, watching him, freeing him from brambles, and protecting him from harm. This gives Jacob the strength to return to his homeland and ask his brother for forgiveness.

Jesus tells us he is the Good Shepherd, that he is personally involved in our life. Jesus is the one who calls us by name and knows us as no one else ever will. He chooses to accompany us on our journey, wherever it leads. When we hear the voice of God we find the direction toward our true self and our true home. We may have other companions and friends on our journey, but only one knows us by name. Jesus leads us to life, to springs of living water, through the gift of his own life.

Oratio

Lord, I hold so much uncertainty in the secret of my heart. I don't know if I can reveal this to anyone. At times I am anxious and insecure. I long for someone to know how I feel and to give me direction. I hear your voice calling my name in the quiet of prayer and the silence of contemplation. I hear you tell me that your love for me is constant. It does not depend on how I feel. Let your voice always resound in my life so that I turn toward you all day long. I entrust the secrets of my heart to you.

Contemplatio

The Lord is my shepherd.

Tuesday of the Fourth Week of Easter

:⋯⋯⋯⋯:

Lectio

John 10:22–30

Meditatio

"No one can take them out of my hand."

Jesus didn't respond to the ultimatums and the timetable of those who demanded to know if he was the messiah. They were looking for easy answers, unwilling to walk the journey of faith and surrender. Because they had already made up their minds, they could not accept it when Jesus told them his true identity: "The Father and I are one."

God does marvels for those who listen to his voice, who follow his invitations and the movements of his Holy Spirit. Saint Paul referred to Jesus' followers as temples of the Spirit. The more receptive we are to his presence and peace, the more we become worthy temples where God is pleased to dwell. No matter our struggles, temptations, or difficulties, God invites us into a deeper relationship with him. God knows us personally, and the more we wholeheartedly seek him, the deeper that relationship will grow.

Human relationships grow when persons communicate with sincerity. Similarly, our relationship with God deepens when we honestly tell him what we think and feel. We never have to be afraid of being ourselves with him, because he knows and accepts us already. God wants us to reveal ourselves to him as we are, not for his sake, but for ours. We need to know that God always loves us unconditionally, just as we are. Not only will God reveal himself to us, but God reveals himself according to our needs.

Jesus promises us: "No one can take them out of my hand." Jesus, the Risen One, is alive and present to us *now*. We can begin to share the experience of his resurrection even in this life, not only after our death. God promises us life in eternity, but he also gives life to our spirit now, everyday. Everyone who sincerely approaches God can trust in his love, for he forever cherishes us.

Oratio

Lord, give me an open ear to listen to your word. Help me to surrender in trust to your plan for me, for I know that your providence guides and permits everything for my good. You invite me to an intimate relationship and hold me in your good hands. Jesus Way, may I follow you as your disciple and lead others to you. Jesus Truth, give me zeal for what is good and true, and a mind that is open to truth. Jesus Life, may your sacraments and the gifts of the Holy Spirit fill me with love that is expressed in acts of justice and charity.

Contemplatio

Jesus, you know me and give me eternal life.

Wednesday of the Fourth Week of Easter

∴∴∴∴∴∴∴∴∴∴∴∴∴

Lectio

John 12:44–50

Meditatio

"I came into the world as light. . . ."

Today's Gospel focuses on one of John's great theme—light! This word has many facets: light is powerful yet gentle, explicit yet mysterious, common yet extraordinary. Jesus identifies himself with light: "I came into the world as light." This proclamation of Jesus' mission communicates a powerful truth—the radiance of Christ will deliver us from darkness and enlighten our journey in life.

I once read that the sun is a giant nuclear fireball radiating energy in all directions. This energy is made visible to the eye as rays of light. We can see everything around us because these rays reflect off objects and into our eyes. If the source of light were obstructed or removed, then the objects would disappear. They wouldn't cease to exist, but they would disappear from our world of sight. Haven't we all tripped over or run into something in a dark room?

Now Jesus announces: "I came into the world as light, so that everyone who believes in me might not remain in darkness." Jesus is like the fireball, radiating energy in every direction—the energy of light and love that penetrates the heart of every person. When we receive this energy, our lives light up, and we ourselves reflect Christ to others.

But if we block out the light of Christ or dim it by our indifference, then the true meaning of life disappears. We continue to exist, but in reality we walk in darkness. We are blinded and cannot see the many ways God reveals himself as light in our lives.

Yet even if we block God's light, he will never cease to diffuse his radiant energy. God invites us to bask in his light. May it penetrate all our actions, and reflect the true light to anyone around us who may still wander in darkness and confusion.

Oratio

Jesus, you are the Light of the World. Yet for some reason I block your light and fumble about in semidarkness as I try to understand what is happening around me. Enlighten my intellect, my desires, and my heart with your light, so that I may follow your ways and walk in the brightness of your love. Lord, I believe in your light; help to dissipate my unbelief and restore your brilliance within me.

Contemplatio

In your light there is life.

Thursday of the Fourth Week of Easter

∴ ·············· ∴

Lectio

John 13:16–20

Meditatio

> *". . . whoever receives the one I send receives me . . ."*

I wonder how easy it was to receive the apostles or disciples, grimy with road dust, hot, tired, and hungry, bearing a message that sounded unbelievable. Was it easy to welcome them? Was it easy to accept their message? I find it amazing that people did come to believe—and in such numbers. In those first years following the resurrection, Christianity spread swiftly throughout the Roman Empire. Only one explanation seems possible: it was a miracle of grace.

If we reflect, we see that our own lives are also marked by grace. We may have received the faith as children from parents and teachers. We may have received it as adults—through books, friends, a counselor or spouse—perhaps after much seeking and soul searching. In any case, how could the faith have come to us except by means of grace?

So, what does the Scripture citation mean for me? I have faith already: who will Jesus send *me* today? Do I still need an apostle or disciple to show me the way?

Well, I really may. I might want to give this some thought. It's also possible, however, that Jesus will send someone for me to help—a needy person like those he searched out during his earthly life and ministry. He may want to continue that ministry through me today.

He may want me to greet a lonely neighbor at my door, an annoying relative on the phone, a physically or mentally challenged stranger in the supermarket, a co-worker in the lunch room whose lifestyle I don't agree with, an acquaintance on the bus whose accent I can hardly understand. He may want me to engage this person in conversation in order to communicate his mercy and unconditional love through me. He probably also wants to communicate to *me* through this *other*, even though the other might not measure up to my concept of a devout and knowledgeable Christian—or might not be a believer at all!

So, am I ready?

Oratio

Lord Jesus, our Teacher and Shepherd, you once said that whatever we do to the least ones we do to you (see Mt 25:40). Help me to remember this when I encounter someone in need. Help me not to be so wrapped up in my own needs, wants, and plans that I can't greet, listen, converse, aid, and learn. Moment by moment, give me the light to see what I am called to say and do. Give me the courage to follow your inspirations. Help me to forget myself more often and focus on you and others instead. Amen.

Contemplatio

Whom might Jesus send me today?

Friday of the Fourth Week of Easter

: • · · · · · · · · · · · · • :

Lectio

John 14:1–6

Meditatio

> ". . . so that where I am you also may be."

This passage marks a transition in John's Gospel. Jesus knows he will no longer be physically accessible to his disciples. But Jesus reveals that they will still have access to him, only in a different way. Through the Holy Spirit, Jesus will be present in his followers, and that presence will be nourished by the Holy Eucharist.

The disciples don't completely understand this. They want to be where Jesus is. Jesus tells them that he will return and take them where he is. And Thomas, speaking for so many of us, says exactly the opposite of what Jesus just said—"but we don't know where you're going, so we don't know the way."

Jesus responds to Thomas in a way completely different from the way the question was posed: no address, no directions. His response is himself. The place that Jesus wants to take us to *is* the Father. He is preparing us for direct contact with the Father. This reality is possible through Jesus alone.

Therefore, the way is wherever Jesus is, because Jesus is always in the presence of the Father. What is the most secure way to the Father? Jesus. Why? Because he reveals the truth about who we are—about the original intent with which the Father created us. By following Jesus, we are able to live as the Father willed that we live before the fall. That is now possible through the life that Jesus won for us, and in which he precedes us as the Risen One.

I am the Way, Jesus says. Walk with me—not around me, not ahead of me. I left you the example. Do what I did because that's the way that will most securely lead you to me. Walk with me because I am the Way. Follow me because I am the Light. I will lead you to life—to my Father, "so that where I am you also may be."

Oratio

Jesus, I struggle with the same thing Thomas did. I want to go to heaven to enjoy the place you are preparing for me. But I'm so unsure how to get there. You tell me that by following in your footsteps I will be with you and with your Father. Help me follow you more closely, especially when I want to go in a different direction. When I am troubled, remind me of the truth that believing you will help me believe in the Father's love for me. May I allow your life to grow in me so that the Father's dream might be fulfilled in me. Amen.

Contemplatio

I can't wait to see the "place" you are preparing for me, Jesus!

Saturday of the Fourth Week of Easter

⋮ ⋯⋯⋯⋯⋯ ⋮

Lectio

John 14:7–14

Meditatio

> *". . . whatever you ask in my name. . . ."*

"Whatever!" How often do you hear this current, non-committal expression? So glib! This is the new all-purpose response. It can be used to affirm, to complain, to bluff, to chase off, to agree when disagreeing and vice versa, to express annoyance or coyness. Whatever! It is a sign of the verbal laziness and the general laissez-faire attitude of our time. Perhaps it has even become your reply of choice. But listen to Christ. When he uses the word, it is specific, defined, and generous: "And whatever you ask in my name, I will do. . . ."

Jesus pumps life and meaning into this word. For him, *whatever* means everything. It is a positive promise, not a verbal ploy. Simply by turning the sentence around we read: I will do whatever you ask in my name. The only stipulation Jesus makes is that we believe he will do whatever he promises, that we affirm his ability to do whatever he wills, and that we accept as true whatever he says. His purpose is that we may have a way of seeing the Father. In Christ, we are able to see the Person of God, hear the words of God, feel the touch of

God. We have seen the goodness, the generosity, the sacrifice, the love of Jesus. He is assuring us that this is a human look at the heart of God. Jesus is giving us a great grace. We have no reason to fear God now that we have been with him all this time. In Christ we have seen his actions and his reactions; we have seen the compassionate face of God.

Oratio

Lord, teach me to be as generous as you are. Teach me the true meaning of self-giving, that I may offer you my fullness, my entire being with an open heart. Whatever you ask of me I will do for you. You show me the heart of the Father, always intent on my good. I thank you for mirroring the divine love for me, for my world. Let me in turn be your face to others, that all may be led to you and see in you the loving face of God.

Contemplatio

"Whoever has seen me has seen the Father."

Sunday of the Fifth Week of Easter — Year A

:·············:

Lectio

John 14:1–12

Meditatio

> *"I am the way . . ."*

It's common for someone to say, "I know the way," or "I can point out the way for you on a map," or even "I can come with you and show you the way." But when someone says, "I don't know the way," who would respond with "*I* am the Way"?

Only Jesus can say this. He himself is the Way. The way to what? The way to the Father, to his Father's house, where Jesus will prepare a place for us. Jesus doesn't just teach people the way to God. He doesn't just give an example of the right way to live. He doesn't just come along as a guide along the way. Jesus does all of these and more.

The first Christians referred to themselves as followers of "the way." Taking Jesus to be our Way is a life-changing decision. God's ways are not our ways, and the Way that is Jesus is very different from the way of the world.

In reading this passage from John's Gospel during the Easter Season, it's easy to forget that the departure Jesus speaks of refers to his imminent passion and death. "Where I am going you know the way." This is the difficult part, for the way includes suffering.

A passage in the book of the prophet Isaiah says: "with your own eyes you shall see your Teacher, while from behind, a voice shall sound in your ears: 'This is the way; walk in it,' when you would turn to the right or to the left" (Is 30:20–21). The prospect of suffering can make us feel that we would rather turn and go a different way. But then the voice of the Holy Spirit whispers in our ears, "No, this is the Way. Follow him."

Oratio

Jesus, I want to follow you wherever you lead me. All paths in life include pain and sorrow at some point—I can't avoid it. We all encounter suffering, no matter how much wealth or power we may have. But when I am with you, I'm not afraid of suffering and darkness and difficulty. You are my Way. Bring me safely to my Father's house.

Contemplatio

This is the way; walk in it.

Sunday of the Fifth Week of Easter — Year B

∴ · · · · · · · · · · · · ∴

Lectio

John 15:1–8

Meditatio

> *"Ask for whatever you want and it will be done for you."*

What a marvelous promise, especially coming from God! When friends ask us what they can do for us, we don't dare request something beyond their capability to give. But this is God asking—and God can give us anything we ask. So why does it seem that our prayers are not always answered? Jesus gives us a clue when he talks about being the true vine in the vineyard of his Father, the Vinedresser.

One year I was in Italy right before the grape harvest, when the vines bore ripe, full grapes. I bit into a grape, and cool sweet juice squirted into my mouth. I asked someone why this vine bore such big, sweet grapes. He explained how the vinedresser pruned the vine, binding drooping tendrils and trimming off branches to focus its growth. Contemplating the grapevine, I realized that "asking for what we will" pre-supposes trusting the Vinedresser. If I had been there when the vinedresser was chopping off branches and tying up tendrils, I may have disagreed with his method. Yet, obviously he knew how to bring an abundant harvest to that vineyard.

The word of God trims us so that we bear fruit. Our fruit grows through life in Christ. Attached to Christ, the true Vine, we feel the sap of Scripture and sacramental life flow toward fruits being formed in our lives. The Spirit of Christ flows through us and in us. Saint Paul writes that we do not know what we ought to pray for, but the Spirit intercedes for us with groans that words cannot express (see Rom 8:26). Jesus says that we glorify God when we bear much fruit. We bear fruit when we trust the Vinedresser and stay attached to Jesus, the true Vine—who is pruned and bears abundant fruit. Through baptism we are incorporated into the true Vine. All that we do is transformed into worship—with Jesus we become Eucharistic grapes squeezed into wine to share with a thirsty world.

Oratio

Jesus, when I cling to you, the true Vine, you transform me. Your life flows through me in the sacraments, in your word, and in prayer. You changed water into wine at the wedding of Cana at the request of Mary. I pray with Saint Paul that it be no longer I who live, but you who live in me (Gal 2:20). May my life flow out toward others as your sweet, vivifying wine.

Contemplatio

The word of God and Eucharistic Communion completely reshape my life.

Sunday of the Fifth Week of Easter — Year C

∴ · · · · · · · · · · · · ∴

Lectio

John 13:31–33a, 34–35

Meditatio

> *"This is how all will know that you are my disciples,*
> *if you have love for one another."*

Imagine yourself as the leader of an association, business, or social group. If you wanted to brand your followers with a sign that would make them easy to recognize, what would you choose? Would they all wear the same clothes? Would they speak a particular language? Would they would be experts at a particular trade or manufacture a unique product?

Jesus did something completely revolutionary. He "branded" his disciples with his very self, but left them free to make him visible by loving others. Saint John says that "God is love" (1 Jn 4:16). Love is the imprint of God's very being upon us, within us. If the world is going to see God, it will only see him to the extent that you and I are willing to make him visible in our relationships with one another. How much do you and I *want* to make God visible?

True, loving one another is a difficult task. It's about living as Jesus did, continually giving our lives away. That's what love does. It goes out of itself in search of the good of the other, so as to give the other life. But it's also about openness to receiving the love God offers us through the other. And that has its challenges too.

The possibilities for *how* to spend the years of our lives or even just the present moment are immense. Jesus invites us to a life of loving one another so that the world might believe, so that he might be made more visible, so that we might be identified as his disciples—branded with love. It's not that we have to tattoo a heart on our arm, but it is as though love is what we wear. Love is what we speak. Love is what we are experts at. Love is what we produce. You can't touch or feel it, but you know he is there.

Oratio

Jesus, you are my Master. I really do want to be recognized as your disciple. Loving others is the path I must walk. Left on my own, the task would be impossible. But you have given us everything we need to make that mutual loving possible. You have given me your Word and the Eucharist to daily nourish your love within me. Your Holy Spirit continually alerts me to the daily opportunities to show your love to others. Help me to be docile to the Spirit's lead.

Contemplatio

Jesus, may all whom I meet today recognize a little bit more of you in me.

Monday of the Fifth Week of Easter

∶⋯⋯⋯⋯∶

Lectio

John 14:21–26

Meditatio

". . . the Holy Spirit . . . will . . . remind you of all that I told you."

Once when I was learning a new job, the sister who was teaching me said about a certain task, "Don't worry. If you forget how to do this, you can ask so-and-so." And about something else, "It's all right if you forget to do that. So-and-so will remind you." It was a relief to know that others would back me up, that I didn't have to do it all on my own, and that I wouldn't ruin everything if I forgot a detail.

Before Jesus leaves his disciples to return to the Father, he reassures them in a similar way. He's taught them many things, and here at this Last Supper especially, he has said a lot. Their hearts and minds can hardly contain it all. But they don't need to be anxious about it. The Holy Spirit will remind them of whatever they need to remember, and will help them learn and apply whatever Jesus has not explained.

This reassures and consoles us, too. We don't need to memorize the Gospels, chapter and verse. We don't need to figure out on our own what it means to follow Jesus, or what a disciple should do in any given situation. It's not all on our shoulders. We have the promise of the Holy Spirit.

What *is* on our shoulders is the duty to be open and to listen so that we hear the Holy Spirit's reminders. We need to ask for assistance when we're not clear about what to do, or how Jesus would want us to act. Praying with the word of God, praying for guidance, turning to ask the Holy Spirit's light, discerning God's will in a certain situation—all these are what *we* need to do. Then the Holy Spirit will remind us of all that Jesus has told us.

Oratio

Jesus, thank you for the gift of your Holy Spirit. Help me trust that I will receive the help I need, when I need it, and then remind me to ask for that help and not rely completely on my own memory and judgment. I place in your hands, right now, all my concerns about the future and about current situations that are not yet clear to me. Send your Holy Spirit to remind me and teach me all I need to know.

Contemplatio

"Do not let your hearts be troubled" (Jn 14:1).

Tuesday of the Fifth Week of Easter

⁘ · · · · · · · · · · · · ⁘

Lectio

John 14:27–31a

Meditatio

> *"If you loved me, you would rejoice*
> *that I am going to the Father."*

This Gospel, a flashback of sorts to the Last Supper, strikes me as a painful reminder of the sorrow of Holy Week. Late in the Easter season, after weeks of alleluias and white lilies, I'd rather not go back to the difficult moments we lived as a Church during the Triduum. The final words of Jesus to his apostles—his closest friends—can be truly heartbreaking.

But as we reread these words of Jesus in light of Easter morning, they take on new meaning. "If you loved me, you would rejoice that I am going to the Father," he says. Putting myself in the apostles' shoes, I wonder how I could be glad to hear Jesus say he is going away. If I loved him, he says, I would be glad. But why? Because, Jesus says, "I love the Father." Jesus' whole life has been about the Father, right up until the very end. He goes to the Father, and promises to return to us, to remain closer to us than ever before.

With these words, Jesus shares with us the mystery of love that is the Trinity. No wonder his words to the apostles are so difficult to understand! But one of the great beauties of this Last Supper passage is that Jesus invites us to share in this great love between him and the Father. Jesus shares with the apostles his deepest reason for his eventual acceptance of Calvary: that the world might see how much he loves the Father. He prepares the apostles (and us) for the experience of the cross and promises the strength we need.

As the celebration of the Ascension approaches, we rejoice in the great love of the Son for the Father, a love so powerful that it leads to our own salvation.

Oratio

Father, I praise you for your amazing love for us in Jesus. May your peace always possess my heart, and may I embrace your will with the freedom and love of Jesus.

Contemplatio

"My peace is my gift to you."

Wednesday of the Fifth Week of Easter

❖ · · · · · · · · · · · · ❖

Lectio

John 15:1–8

Meditatio

"You are the branches."

When I read through the Bible, even if I just flip the pages a bit, I am sure to find a reference to a vine or vineyard. Having a vineyard of one's own seems to have been ancient Israel's equivalent of the "American dream." In a way, cultivating a flourishing vineyard takes more work than building a house. The vine, after all, is a living thing. And throughout the Scriptures, the cherished "vineyard of the LORD of hosts is the house of Israel" (Is 5:7), the whole Chosen People.

That is what makes today's Gospel stand out: Jesus says that he is "the" Vine, the "true" Vine. Whereas the prophets imagined the vineyard of Israel being given up entirely to destruction for failing to bear good fruit, Jesus says that only the fruitless branches of this vine will be cast away. The others will also feel the sting of the garden shears, but only for a life-giving pruning that guarantees a good harvest. What is important, then, is that the branches of this true vine bear fruit. The branches extend the presence of the life-giving vine beyond the confines of its stem; it is only through the branches that the vine can bear fruit! Saint Paul wasn't talking about a vine, but he did write about the "fruits of the Spirit": charity, joy, peace, patience. . . (see Gal 5:22). Those fruits become the much-needed sign that Jesus is very much alive and present in our world today.

Oratio

Lord, I can't even imagine a vine without branches. What would it be? It would be a gnarled stem, unable to spread and fill the vineyard with color and fragrance. So I understand you to tell me that I am already living in deep communion with you, and that all I have to do is remain with you, in you, and in your word. Your life in me will do the rest, making my words and actions bear fruits of life for those around me.

Contemplatio

The Lord says, "Because of me you bear fruit!" (Hos 14:9).

Thursday of the Fifth Week of Easter

⁖ · · · · · · · · · · · · ⁖

Lectio

John 15:9–11

Meditatio

> *"I have told you this so that my joy might be in you
> and your joy might be complete."*

Taken out of context, John's chapter 15 is simply one of the loveliest passages in the Bible. But put into perspective it becomes both stunningly gorgeous and gut-wrenchingly painful at the same time. Jesus sits at table with his disciples. They must sense the tensions that surround the Master, but do they realize what events will unfold on that evening and the following day? Jesus stands on the brink of his passion and death, and he speaks of joy being complete. Eighteen hours later, these words will seem ironic at best.

"As the Father loves me, so I also love you. . . ." In the short run this love doesn't look so inviting. The Father has sent the Son on what looks like a wild goose chase after God's wayward people. Jesus' whole ministry is about to come crashing down, ending brutally on the cross. The Father's love has set the Son an impossible task—or so it seems—yet he sits here talking about his joy being complete?

But Christ is risen. The fact of the resurrection changes everything. The complete self-emptying of the Son is met by the complete outpouring of the Father and the Spirit. In the mystery of the Trinity, death and chaos cannot bind Jesus because his life is held, sustained, and honored by the Father and Spirit. This is life—true life—that does not decay or come to an end.

This incredible gift of God's life is shared with us in baptism. "As the Father loves me, so I also love you." In the end death and chaos have no permanent hold on us, either. We are in Christ. Given this knowledge, the confidence and joy that pulsate in the words of Jesus in this Gospel become our joy. This joy is complete.

Oratio

Lord, your love persistently waits for a response. You want us to live in your love; to remain with you. Day after day you repeat this invitation. Day after day you nourish us with your words and with the Eucharist. Let me enter into your *joie de vivre*, to deal with people and approach situations with your perspective. Live in me, so that my presence brings grace and consolation. Live in me, so that I may live in you.

Contemplatio

". . . so that my joy might be in you . . ."

Friday of the Fifth Week of Easter

⁘ ⋯⋯⋯⋯ ⁘

Lectio

John 15:12–17

Meditatio

> *"I no longer call you slaves . . . I have called you friends, because I have told you everything. . . ."*

We are not slaves of Jesus, but his friends. So why, in the previous line, does he say, "you are my friends if you do what I command you"? That's a little confusing. Don't slaves do what they're commanded to do? But Jesus explains that a slave isn't "in on" the master's plans. Slaves do what they're told without any understanding of the bigger picture, of what part they play, or what the goal is.

Friends are different. We can tell things to our friends and share our plans with them. Think back to friends from childhood. Even then, friends were kids we shared things with—secrets, fears, hopes, and dreams. Adult friendships are different in many ways, but it's still true that our friends are those we can confide in and, of course, who *want* to listen to what we tell them: "Tell me everything!" For some friends, that's as far as it goes—they're "emotional support." But for others, it goes deeper.

Jesus wants friends who not only know about the plan and the goal, but who also pitch in and work toward the goal.

Jesus doesn't tell us what he has "heard from the Father" just so we can cheer him on. He invites us to join him. "You are my friends if you do what I command you."

It starts with loving one another, his first command to us. Love is the foundation of the community of his friends. Then he sends us to bear fruit. That is what it means to be friends of Jesus.

Oratio

Jesus, I love to hear you call me your friend. I don't want to be a fair-weather friend who sticks by you only as long as the plan is going well. I don't want to be your friend in name only. I want to be a true friend who is close to you and hears all that you share with me.

Sometimes it's hard for me to love these others whom you also call your friends. But I know that that is the indispensible first step. First we must love each other; then we can work on your plan to make the love of your Father known to every human being.

Contemplatio

I am a friend of Jesus.

Saturday of the Fifth Week of Easter

❖ · · · · · · · · · · · · ❖

Lectio

John 15:18–21

Meditatio

> "... *I have chosen you out of the world.*"

As I enter into this Gospel scene in my imagination, Lord, I place myself among your disciples. I too consider myself your disciple. I want to learn your way; I want to be with you, to be like you, to understand your teaching so that I can share it with others. As I listen to you speak, I hear you talk to me directly. You are instructing us, your disciples. You are speaking with a kind of rhythm, almost a musical cadence, that easily draws me in. "If you . . . then . . . me . . ." and again, "If . . . me. . . then you . . ." You are linking us inextricably together. You are affirming that we are now in this life together, you and I, inseparably.

It reminds me of your startling words to Saul before he became Saint Paul, words that so completely caught him off-guard that they entirely enraptured him. He was on that famous road to Damascus, intent on carrying out further persecutions against your people, the newly named Christians. You said to him, "Saul, Saul, why are you persecuting me?" (Acts 9:4) In a revelation that astounded him, you identified yourself personally with the Christians whom Saul was persecuting. That identification was so real that by persecuting them, Saul was actually persecuting you. You were one with those Christians, and they were one with you in their suffering.

I often say that I desire to be like you, Lord, yet this is far too little compared with what you desire for me. Your desire to be united to your disciples is so powerful and profound that far more than becoming *like* you, you enable us to become *one with you.* You did this, for Saint Paul could say, ". . . yet I live, no longer I, but Christ lives in me" (Gal 2:20). By uniting yourself to us in this way, you give us courage and all the strength we need to meet life's challenges. I am not alone in any of the sufferings I endure in your name—you are with me, and together we can handle them.

Oratio

May my life become a means of encounter with you, Lord, for all the people that I meet. Seeing me, may they see you. And if they are not able to accept me, or if they are unkind in any way, let me unite myself even more deeply to you, Lord, asking your mercy for them. Let me forgive them as you would forgive them, Lord, and love them as you would love them.

Contemplatio

You have chosen me, Lord, and I am choosing you.

Sunday of the Sixth Week of Easter — Year A

Lectio

John 14:15–21

Meditatio

> "... I will love him and reveal myself to him."

The promises Jesus makes in today's Gospel are very consoling! To show how much he tenderly cares for us, Jesus uses the image of a defenseless orphan who needs protection. In the Hebrew tradition, the king was supposed to protect the rights of the poor and powerless. God protects us, too, in our poverty, in whatever ways we experience our weakness.

God is drawn to our vulnerability when we open the wounded areas of our hearts. God's life-giving grace sustains us when we feel helpless. Our very helplessness draws down God's strength! For this reason, when we lay bare our sin and weakness to God's healing presence, he strengthens and heals us. The Holy Spirit, the Advocate sent by the Father, always pleads for us and lifts us up in hope. The evil spirit, instead, condemns and weighs us down with the sadness of sin.

Jesus links our fidelity in following God's commandments with our capacity to receive grace and the gifts of the Holy Spirit. Following Jesus' way of love is essential in developing a deeper relationship with God. The Holy Trinity's indwelling is pure gift. Yet, in a mysterious way, we open ourselves to this gift as we try to live the commandments and the beatitudes. The more receptive our hearts, the more God will satisfy our longing for communion with him.

God's indwelling presence intensifies within us when we live consistently with our Christian vocation. Sin not only weighs us down and saddens us, it makes us less open to truth, goodness, and beauty. Sin makes us less aware and responsive to the needs of others, and increasingly self-preoccupied. Those who sincerely try to follow Jesus will find not only that truth is more transparent to them, but that God's Spirit gives them the strength to live as Christian disciples, especially when the cost of discipleship is high. Their relationship with God will grow more intimate, and they will experience God's presence more intensely.

Oratio

Holy Trinity, communion of Father, Son, and Holy Spirit, I am humbled to be your temple. Thank you for living in my heart and for inviting me to be your disciple. Jesus, you are my Master and Teacher. Help me to better live your truth and to speak your truth to a waiting world. Give me the grace to live the beatitudes both in my home and my workplace, so that I may make a difference in a world broken by sorrow. May your word and sacraments be the life-giving springs that nourish me and help me view everyone with your loving eyes.

Contemplatio

Jesus, you love me; reveal yourself to me, live in me.

Sunday of the Sixth Week of Easter — Year B

Lectio

John 15:9–17

Meditatio

> *"Remain in my love."*

Jesus is in the upper room with his apostles. In a little while he will lay down his life for them, but they don't understand. Jesus doesn't talk too much about what is going to happen to him. Rather, he is concerned about how his disciples will cope with his death.

So what does Jesus do? He invites them to remain in his love—to make his love their permanent dwelling place. The love of the Father is *his* permanent dwelling place. Nothing and no one can change that—not even his impending death. But his disciples must know that the Father's love is meant to be their permanent dwelling place too.

Imagine! Jesus invites us to "hang out" *in his love*. Have you ever thought about where you regularly hang out *interiorly*? We actually might have several interior hangouts. Perhaps we dwell in guilt, anxiety, fear, resentment, self-preoccupation, or concern about what others think of us. In those places, our mind feeds on negative thoughts and our hearts are held captive to emotions that keep us closed in on self and unaware of God and those around us.

Jesus offers us another hangout, a place of real security no matter what the situation is around us. That place is in the Father's love. What would my day look like if I really *remained* in the Father's love? Might I be on the lookout for all the creative ways he was using to show me his love: the sunrise, the hot cup of coffee in the morning, the reassuring word of a friend, the difficult task I was able to finish, the coworker who apologized to me for a misunderstanding that happened days ago? Might I "run into his love" when I felt hurt, rejected, like a failure, misunderstood? Might I think of him more often during the day and try to find ways to let that love flow through me to others? Hanging out in the Father's love could totally change my life!

Oratio

Jesus, you are inviting me to remain in your love. I want so much to do that, yet some things hold me back. Give me courage to surrender, to let go of my need to be in control, to be right, to be Number 1. Only then will I truly be able to remain in your love.

Contemplatio

Jesus, live in me so that I may live in you.

Sunday of the Sixth Week of Easter — Year C

Lectio

John 14:23–29

Meditatio

> *"Whoever loves me will keep my word. . . ."*

Often we check off the box next to this passage, saying to ourselves, "Of course, no problem." We keep the word. We have Bibles and missals with the word in them. In fact, these books have places of honor in our homes. But, when Christ says, "keep my word," he doesn't mean to keep it in a display case—as a holy dust collector, the sacred record book of all the family sacraments. No, he means to keep it as we keep the commandments. It's not simply that we don't break the commandments, or lose the word, but that we live them. Just as the commandments summarize who we are as believers, so the word is how we live our Christ-in-us, our baptismal consecration. The important words are *is* and *are*. These words are active, alive, present. *The commandments summarize who we are. The word is how we live.* In this passage of John, Christ speaks of a living relationship; it is love—the exchange between us. Look at what Christ promises if we live his word: the Father will come to us, live in us, and make his dwelling within us.

The Holy Spirit, who is the bond of love between the Father and the Son, will also come to live in us. The Spirit brings the gift of peace, our heart's greatest longing. Living with God's word gives us great peace. It dissipates all trouble and fear, and envelops us in rejoicing. We will experience it as the shepherds did who heard the message from the angels when Christ was born: ". . . and on earth peace to those on whom his favor rests" (Lk 2:14). The Spirit will keep God's word for us, within us, reminding us how to live it in love.

Oratio

Dear Lord, I want to be a keeper. I want your word to live within me. Open my eyes to your presence, my ears to your word, so that I will live in awareness of my relationship with you. I invite you, I welcome you, Father, Son, and Holy Spirit, to dwell within me, so that I may be an expression of your presence in love and peace within the world.

Contemplatio

Your word is my life.

Monday of the Sixth Week of Easter

⋮ · · · · · · · · · · · · ⋮

Lectio

John 15:26–16:4a

Meditatio

"When the Advocate comes whom I will send you from the Father. . . ."

All of us are bound to get into some sort of trouble during our lives. When we face an adversary who accuses us of something, we need an advocate. At such times it's consoling to know that someone will come to our aid and help us out of the trouble we have gotten into. In today's Gospel Jesus tells his apostles quite plainly to expect trouble. If we profess faith in Jesus, we will meet opposition. Jesus even tells the apostles that they could get killed on his account. And we know from Church history that most of the apostles did give their lives for him as martyrs. But Jesus' warning came with a promise. He promised to send the Advocate, the Holy Spirit, who will come to our aid at such times of crisis. The Holy Spirit will sustain us as our Advocate.

This Gospel can help us reflect on the question: How do I look on God? Do I see him as a judge who is always on the lookout for anything I do wrong? Or do I see him as he really is—our Advocate? Difficult experiences in life, especially when we are children, can color our image of God. We might see him as a severe father who is never pleased with our efforts, no matter how hard we try. Or we might see him as someone distant and uncaring who doesn't want to be bothered with us at all.

But if we see God as our Advocate, it changes our outlook. God wants us to succeed, and helps us to do it. If we fail or get into trouble, we can go confidently to our Advocate for help in straightening out the situation. God is always sending us love. Sometimes it can be a tough love that makes demands on us so that we don't fall into an easy mediocrity. God always wants the best for us and asks only for our trust. Are we willing?

Oratio

Lord Jesus, help me to trust you. At times it's easy to slip into a false way of thinking that prevents me from truly believing that you love me. But you tell us to come to you with confidence. You even sent the Holy Spirit as our Advocate. I turn to you with faith. Help me to trust your love, never doubting it for one second.

Contemplatio

Jesus, I trust in you.

Tuesday of the Sixth Week of Easter

❖ · · · · · · · · · · · · ❖

Lectio

John 16:5–11

Meditatio

> ". . . it is better for you that I go."

Jesus seems to leave his disciples in the lurch when he tells them, ". . . it is better for you that I go." They wonder why after leaving everything to answer his call to "come and follow me," he is now saying, "you cannot come." Earlier Peter had asked: "Master, where are you going?" Jesus assured Peter by saying, "Do not let your hearts be troubled. You have faith in God; have faith also in me" (Jn 14:1). Thomas pushed the question a little further. He reminded Jesus that they didn't know where he was going. How could they know the way? This question prompted Jesus' wonderful self-definition: "I am the way and the truth and the life" (Jn 14:6). In chapter 16 of John's Gospel the disciples are no longer asking Jesus where he is going or why he must go. Grief has filled their hearts.

There will be times in our life of faith when Jesus seems to disappear and nothing makes sense. Perhaps these are times when our understanding of God is being purified. Our longing for God increases as we descend into this unknowing. Our love of God is growing beyond our limited understanding of God's ways. We enter a trial of trust only because God has great trust in us. The disciples dreamed big dreams. They hoped to sit at the right and left of Jesus when he entered his kingdom. They had to let go of their image of the Messiah, for Jesus' promise is so much bigger than they could imagine. The Spirit, the love of the Father and the Son, will reveal it to them in the depths of their being.

In the *Divine Comedy*, when Dante enters heaven, Saint John the Apostle asks him whom he loves and why. The Spirit helps us refine our answer, proving the world wrong about sin, about justice, about condemnation, by revealing the truth of who we are and the truth of God's great love.

Oratio

Send us your Spirit, Lord. You do not leave us alone; your Spirit abides with us and in us. Thank you, Holy Spirit, for being my companion and healer during my pilgrimage of life. Bring your light into the night of my soul, and breathe your life anew in me every day.

Contemplatio

Come, Holy Spirit!

Wednesday of the Sixth Week of Easter

❖ · · · · · · · · · · · · ❖

Lectio

John 16:12-15

Meditatio

> "*. . . the Spirit of truth . . . will guide you to all truth . . . and will declare to you the things that are coming . . .*"

If we are to be guided to the truth and if the Holy Spirit will "declare" the "things that are coming," then it is good to know what to expect. What could "the things that are coming" be? This phrase reminded me of the way that the Jews spoke about the Messiah—he is the "one who is to come" (see Lk 7:20). This, along with Jesus' statement in John 14:6 that he is the Truth, leads me to a conclusion: I believe that the "truth" the Spirit guides us to, and the things that are coming that he will declare to us, are actually the person of Jesus.

It is our glory as human beings to be able to be guided to *all* truth. We do not perceive this truth abstractly, the way we perceive other truths. No, this truth is a person—and we are able to embrace this truth through a spiritual reality called grace.

The Spirit is the bond of unity in the Trinity. That bond has a name: Love. The Spirit is the perfect lover. It is as a lover that he guides us to all truth—the Person of Jesus, who in turn reveals the Person of His Father. As a perfect lover, the Spirit reveals only as much as we are capable of receiving. He knows the right way to touch us, where to touch us, when to touch us. He knows when we are ready and just how much light we can take. As fear melts away in the presence of a person who truly loves us, so our fear melts because the Spirit, the Revealer, loves us perfectly. When we allow the Spirit to accomplish his mission in us, God is glorified, not only through the Spirit, but in our beings as well.

Oratio

Spirit of Truth, you are love personified. You want to communicate to me love, truth, and the things that are coming. These three realities have a name: Jesus. Prepare me to receive the "things that are coming." Remove the blinders that cover my eyes, that I may see the truth. Teach me to perceive the truth you impart. Grant me the courage to transform my life so that I can become a vessel of divine life. I want to be able to do this in the measure that Mary did. Then I too will be able to glorify God for the marvels he has done in me. Amen.

Contemplatio

I await your gift of truth, O Spirit; I long to hear what you have to declare!

Thursday of the Sixth Week of Easter[*]

∙∙∙∙∙∙∙∙∙∙∙∙∙∙∙

Lectio

John 16:16–20

Meditatio

". . . your grief will become joy."

When the Gospel writer refers to the "world" in today's reading, he does not mean that God's creation or the people in our world are evil. All that God creates and sustains is good. Instead, the "world" refers to a spirit that is prone to pride, greed, and sin. Such a worldly spirit is indifferent to the needs and suffering of others and is centered on its own gratification. A godly spirit, instead, is compassionate and responds to injustice and the needs of neighbors. God's Spirit leads us to be more attuned to God's action in our life and in the lives of others.

God is a master at turning sorrow into joy, or at least peace. He is the heart's healer. The Holy Spirit will gently heal our every sorrow and loss. We need only to open our hearts patiently to his gentle and healing action. Yes, feelings of grief and sorrow may persist for a long time, but God promises us enough grace to sustain us on the way of our Christian journey. And that is all that we need. God's grace will bind up our hearts. Nothing is wasted or lost in our faith journey. Every loss can help us to become more sensitive to the sufferings of others and to reach out in empathy and action.

Every difficult moment in our life is an opportunity for the Holy Spirit to transform our lives as he infuses his gifts into our hearts. While we would never choose to suffer, we can grow through these events. God's providence strengthens us through the suffering and can bring unexpected good into our lives. God leads us to greater trust as we seek to embrace what we cannot always understand.

Oratio

Gracious God, your dream for me is always a good dream, one more vast than I can see for myself. Your care has shielded me in the past, and embraces my present and every moment of my future. Your providence for me is so much more than I could ever imagine. You always have my greater good at heart, and you invite me to wait patiently for your plan to unfold. Give me the hope I need to go on when my understanding is unclear. Jesus, I believe that if I trust in you, you will help me in everything.

Contemplatio

"Let me see you, let me hear your voice . . ." (Sg 2:14)

---

* See pages 106–111 for the Ascension of the Lord.

Friday of the Sixth Week of Easter

:⋯⋯⋯:

Lectio

John 16:20–23

Meditatio

> *"On that day you will not question me about anything."*

On *that* day . . . and not before! I picture Jesus saying this with a twinkle in his eye, because he knows that from the minute that our minds kick into gear until the moment we draw our last breath, we will be asking questions.

Banish the thought of the serene mystic sitting in her cell contemplating with great tranquility the movements of the Spirit. Christian life is tough and sometimes downright problematic. The worldly can fritter away their time and energy and dull their anxieties in cheap entertainment and quick-fix pleasures. "Amen, amen, I say to you, you will weep and mourn, while the world rejoices. . . ." The follower of Christ simply cannot evade the great questions for long.

Live fully present in this world with your heart attuned to God's heart, and you will be torn by the sight of so much suffering and ignorance. Why do the just suffer? Why are children robbed of their innocence? Why is the gift of life bought and sold like a commodity? Why is forgiveness next to impossible? Why? Why? Why? Prayers of petition and acts of compassion come from seeing these things. And while, deep down, we may feel a peace that the world cannot touch or understand, suffering still unsettles us. The Lord speaks of anguish with reason.

But the day will come when all questions will be answered. It is, in fact, already mysteriously here in the person of Jesus Christ. Death and decay do not have the last word. The last word is life. Christ is risen and has given us his life. Our resurrection in Christ is a future event that has in one sense already happened, and in another sense is still being worked out. We live in an in-between time. We wait in hope for the day of rejoicing.

Oratio

Lord, you promise that when we see you again our hearts will rejoice completely; all anxiety and questions will disappear. I cannot wait for that day—and yet I must wait for it to come. Teach me to hold fast to the life you have won for us by your passion, death, and resurrection. Let your Spirit work in my response to the suffering and limitations that I see around me and within me. Let your Spirit move me to prayer and petition.

Contemplatio

The answer is Jesus Christ.

Saturday of the Sixth Week of Easter

:⋯⋯⋯⋯:

Lectio

John 16:23b–28

Meditatio

> *". . . ask and you will receive."*

In some way, every human story can be traced back to the Garden of Eden, to that crucial moment when Adam and Eve reached out their hands and grasped the forbidden fruit. Deceived by the serpent, they saw that the fruit was desirable, and so they ate it. But the real moment of sin came right before that, at the moment when they doubted God's word. They doubted that God wanted the best for them. They doubted his love for them and believed the lie that they could only get what they needed if they took it for themselves. Their grasping contained the root of every sin that would stain the pages of human history.

In today's Gospel Jesus offers us the remedy for sin. Instead of grasping, he tells us, all we have to do is ask for what we need, and we will receive it. It's as simple as that. As if to reassure our doubting hearts, he tells us plainly, "The Father himself loves you." Because God loves us, we can trust that he wants what is best for us and will give it to us. God is Gift, and we receive our life and very being from him as a gift. Everything we receive in life is a gift, and we need only receive those gifts gratefully. This doesn't mean to be passive, of course, for we can and should actively work to develop ourselves. But it does mean that we can relax and trust that God's providence will always provide.

When I want something, God may ask me to probe my motives to uncover what I'm really seeking. Do I want this thing for some selfish reason? Or do I want it so that I can make a gift of myself? I will find happiness and fulfillment to the extent that I am generous in making a self-gift.

Oratio

Lord, put my desires in order. Help me to desire those things that you want for me, those things that are truly for my good. I trust you. Thank you for all the wonderful gifts you have poured into my life. Give me eyes that see your goodness everywhere. And help me to be generous in sharing your gifts with others.

Contemplatio

Lord, I believe in your love for me.

Ascension of the Lord*—
Year A

:·············:

Lectio

Matthew 28:16–20

Meditatio

> ". . . they worshiped, but they doubted. . . ."

This Gospel contains a puzzle some commentators seem to overlook. The scene comes after the resurrection. In response to Jesus' command, the eleven disciples have gone to a mountain in Galilee to meet him. And "when they saw him, they worshiped, but they doubted. Then Jesus approached and said to them, 'All power . . .'"

Wait a minute. How could the apostles have truly worshiped Jesus at the same time that "they doubted"? And why doesn't Jesus seem to notice? He simply approaches the eleven disciples and, although he knows the limits of their faith, he gives them unlimited authority! "All power in heaven and on earth has been given to me. Go, therefore, and make disciples. . . ." That quite literally means *all* power—there is no power outside of what Jesus has been given. But to be clear, he even specifies, "all power in heaven and on earth. . . ."

And what does Jesus do with all this power? He commissions the apostles, investing them with an authority far beyond what anyone else could give them—unrestricted authority to baptize, to teach, and to make disciples of all nations. Yet Jesus knows who these men are, these men who are worshipers and doubters at the same time. Even now, after accompanying Jesus, listening to his teachings, seeing miracles, witnessing his passion, death, and astounding resurrection—after all this, they still doubt him.

Jesus doesn't hesitate to commission the still imperfect eleven disciples. He doesn't fear what they will do with this newly invested authority because he is not leaving them alone. "I am with you always, until the end of the age." These are among the most consoling words of Scripture. Jesus addresses these words to his disciples and to us. We would have reason to fear our many imperfections if we were left to ourselves, but we have the Lord's promise, "I am with you always, until the end of the age."

Oratio

Lord, I desire to trust you in all things, because you truly are the all-powerful one. Instead, my many attempts at control betray my doubts that you will really be there for me. I am confident that you also desire me to be your disciple in spite of my imperfections. Help me look for your presence in my daily life with confident trust, because I am sure you are with me always.

Contemplatio

Lord, I trust in you; increase my trust.

---

* See page 112 for the Seventh Sunday of Easter.

Ascension of the Lord —
Year B

❖ · · · · · · · · · · · · ❖

Lectio

Mark 16:15–20

Meditatio

> *". . . they went forth and preached everywhere,*
> *while the Lord worked with them . . ."*

Lent looms large in a Catholic's spiritual terrain, with its various penances and prayers, culminating in the drama of Holy Week and the jubilant alleluias of Easter. For me, however, all of this is only a prelude to the feast of the Ascension. I wait for this day expectantly every year.

At Christmas we celebrate God-with-us. On Good Friday we mourn our sin, because of which we were purchased at the price of Jesus' death. On Easter we sing "Alleluia!" and rejoice at Jesus risen from the tomb. But on the Ascension we marvel that in Christ we are already seated at the right hand of God. We contemplate the designs of the Father's love who wanted us to be part of the Trinity's life and love forever. In Christ—God and man—we are inserted into the communion of the Trinity, we who are but dust and ashes. It would be like Bill Gates giving his entire fortune to a homeless person, inviting him into his family as his heir and dearest son. We are that homeless person who has been given the divine inheritance full and entire, as a gift, obtained through the obedience of Christ. We have been named the dearest, newest member of the family.

This reading from Mark helps us realize the larger picture in which we live out our lives as Catholics. We cannot take up the divine inheritance won for us and then live for ourselves. Jesus says: go out, preach the Gospel, baptize. We are commissioned to make this family of God grow. It's not ultimately about me, but about the delirious joy of making it possible for as many others as possible to receive what we have been given. The Lord works with us as we proclaim this outlandish love of God to others. Ultimately, this is the greatest thing we can do with our lives.

Oratio

Jesus, I have to admit that I rarely consider my life to be mainly about what you have destined for me, to be at your right hand for all eternity. I have family members and friends for whom this is hardly a consideration at all. Life here and now, problems and difficulties, wealth and enjoyment, so many things conspire to steal our focus . . . after all, we are but dust and ashes. But I know you realize that. Right now, today, I thank you for all you have given me by your life, death, and resurrection, and I adore you seated at the right hand of God, where you are saving a place for me.

Contemplatio

May everyone know you and love you, Lord Jesus.

Ascension of the Lord — Year C

∴ · · · · · · · · · · · · ∴

Lectio

Luke 24:46–53

Meditatio

> *"Then he led them out as far as Bethany,*
> *raised his hands, and blessed them."*

Boston's Storrow Drive has a sign that reads "reverse curve" to alert drivers to an unexpected twist in the road. At some point an ardent fan changed it to "reverse the curse," referring to the superstition that Babe Ruth had cursed the Red Sox when they sold him to the Yankees. But when the Red Sox won the World Series in 2004 after a drought of 86 years, jubilant fans cheered that the "curse" had been broken.

We can laugh at such superstitious curses. The Bible, however, speaks of a more sinister curse, the curse of sin. That curse fell on the world when our first parents turned away from God and ushered in the long reign of sin and death. But today's feast of the Ascension gives us cause to celebrate, for Jesus has fully conquered sin. He has truly "reversed the curse" that fell on the world as a result of Adam's sin. The Ascension is the last stage of the work that Jesus came on earth to do. Through his passion and death, resurrection and ascension, Jesus conquered sin and redeemed the world. He returned to the Father, mission accomplished. The Gospel emphasizes this by noting how Jesus raised his hands in blessing: "As he blessed them he parted from them and was taken up to heaven."

The blessing of Jesus, his final gift to us, touches us whenever we need it. He pours into us the grace we need to live as his disciples. We have not yet reached the finish line, so we still struggle with sin and face all kinds of difficulties. But Jesus stays with us through it all. We are not cursed, we are blessed, and for that we rejoice. Our rejoicing today is not that of jubilant sports fans savoring a fleeting moment of victory, but the rejoicing of those who know that in Jesus we have won the only victory that really matters.

Oratio

Jesus, sometimes when I look at the world it seems like sin still has the upper hand. Poverty, abortion, corruption, family breakdowns, and so many other evils seem to be increasing. I can get discouraged and think my small efforts to do good are useless. In those moments, Lord, help me to remember that you have already won the final victory over sin and death. You have blessed all of us and continue to bless us every day. Show us your power and help us to always live in the joy of your resurrection and ascension.

Contemplatio

Lord, pour out your blessing on us.

Sunday of the Seventh Week of Easter — Year A

∴· · · · · · · · · · · ·∴

Lectio

John 17:1–11a

Meditatio

> *"Now this is eternal life, that they should know you,*
> *the only true God. . . ."*

These words express the faith of the Church, rooted in such Scriptures as ". . . we shall see him as he is" (1 Jn 3:2), and "Then I shall know fully, as I am fully known" (1 Cor 13:12). Down through the centuries, philosophers and theologians have delved into the mystery of the God who revealed himself in Jesus Christ. Some of them have used the term "beatific vision" to describe what the blessed enjoy—a face-to-face experience of God himself. The blessed behold the majestic God whom we call "Father," who also manifests the gentleness of a mother.

What is God like?

We, with our earthly limitations, cannot answer that. But we might try to respond to another question: "What would life in God's presence be like? What would I see and feel?" Pause a moment, close your eyes, and wonder . . . and ponder . . . and imagine. . . .

Warmth and color, light and music, the sensation of floating, of soaring, of swimming in a balmy sea, of being held in a gentle embrace.... No matter what we envision, it's earthbound, for we can't imagine what we've never experienced. Saint Paul wrote that no eyes have ever seen, no ears have ever heard, no mind has ever imagined what God has ready for the people who love him (see I Cor 2:9).

The same is true of the name "Father." Some of us can resonate with that name because of our own positive experiences. But God is far more wonderful than the best of human parents. How do we know? Because Jesus lived his entire life on earth totally for the Father. He said that his food was to do the Father's will (see Jn 4:34).

Oratio

Lord Jesus Christ, you taught us to call God "Father." Help me to think of him not as a parent with limitations and failings, but as an all-wise and all-good father. The Gospels have given me glimpses of your tender love for him, with whom you were in continual communication. Doing the Father's will was your food. Help me to imitate you and grow in love for him. Inspire writers and producers of the media to spread the message of the Father's love. Grant that in the next life we may all live in his presence, forever growing in knowledge, love, and joy.

Contemplatio

"... children of God ... so we are" (I Jn 3:1).

Sunday of the Seventh Week of Easter — Year B

:⋯⋯⋯•

Lectio

John 17:11b–19

Meditatio

> *"They do not belong to the world
> any more than I belong to the world."*

Jesus prays to his Father for his disciples: "They do not belong to the world any more than I belong to the world." But on this earthly journey it is so easy to get trapped in what belongs to the world, what is secure and comfortable. We're bombarded by endless advertisements that promise us happiness if we only "eat these foods, wear these clothes, use these lotions." But these products certainly do not determine who I am or what I am called to be. Jesus' message brings me back to reality and reminds me that life goes beyond material things. His message leads me to a way of life that is founded on something deeper and eternal, on virtues that can even touch the lives of others. Such virtues can turn the world's standards upside down.

I experienced this once when I was young. My parents had signed me up for piano lessons. After a few months of classes the teacher asked me to play in a recital for family and friends. I diligently practiced my chosen musical score. Finally, the day arrived. When my name was called, I walked toward the piano, sat on the bench, and panicked. My fingers froze, the music was a blur, and my musical abilities seemed to have disappeared. I uselessly tried to pound out a few notes. Then the tears began to flow down my cheeks, and it was over. But the audience gave me a standing ovation. According to the standards of success and musical talent, I had failed. But the people in that room did not let these standards condition their deeper values of love, support, and compassion.

How often we find ourselves in situations when we need to separate ourselves from worldly expectations or pressures and to choose what is true, loving, and hopeful—to choose what is of God. For this, Jesus added to his prayer a powerful request: "Consecrate them in the truth."

Oratio

Jesus, teach me to pray as you pray. Often my prayers are said in desperation for personal needs. I know you are pleased even with these requests, but as I listen to you pray I witness a prayer of adoration to the Heavenly Father and of gratitude for all that he permits. It is a universal prayer, one that leads to the real reason for lifting our minds and hearts to you: to be consecrated in the truth.

Contemplatio

"Consecrate them in the truth, your word is truth."

Sunday of the Seventh Week of Easter — Year C

:•·············•:

Lectio

John 17:20–26

Meditatio

> *"And I have given them the glory you gave me,*
> *so that they may be one, as we are one. . . ."*

"I have given them the glory you gave me. . . ." God's initiative is to gift us with his glorious life. The first move is grace: ". . . so that they may be one as we are one." God is Trinity: a communion of three persons in perfect unity. The uniqueness of each divine person is cherished, and the harmony is complete and beyond our comprehension. It is a mystery about which the likes of Saint Augustine and Saint Basil have written and taught eloquently, and before which they found themselves humbled.

This is the communion and unity that we are called to live in the Church. It is a mystery, yet a very real thing we grapple with throughout life. I find myself wrestling periodically with this message of God. My experience of community is that it is a wonderful, complicated, messy thing. There are seasons when I feel myself buoyed up by the prayers and example of my local community. The joys of my sisters are my joys; their creativity inspires me, their weaknesses call forth my compassion. But more often than I'd like to admit, an undercurrent of annoyance rumbles around in my consciousness. Life would be so much more wonderful if Sister X would only get her act together, or if Sister Y would grow up. And would somebody please do something about Sister Z!

I suspect that the microcosm of the convent is not unique—hang around "coffee and doughnuts" in a parish long enough, or read any Church history book, and you'll find factions, heresies, sex scandals, embezzlement, and other misdeeds. We are the very human Body of Christ. Yet, we *are* the Body of Christ. The priestly prayer of Jesus pulls us out of our limited existential reality and puts us in the realm of mystery. God is Trinity. God is community, and he invites us into his life of communion/community.

Oratio

Jesus, you came to us through Mary's yes, conceived of the Holy Spirit and born into a human family: a community of mother, father, and child. Later, you called Peter, John, Andrew . . . you started a community of disciples. At the Last Supper you prayed that we all might be one as you and the Father are one. Your Spirit descended on the disciples as they were joined *together* in prayer. Community is part of the DNA of Christianity. The strength of this call is in your initiative of grace, not in our human weakness. Help me to view my community with compassion, with your perspective of grace.

Contemplatio

One *in* Christ Jesus

Monday of the Seventh Week of Easter

∵ · · · · · · · · · · · ∵

Lectio

John 16:29–33

Meditatio

"Now you are talking plainly. . . ."

At the Last Supper the disciples say they believe Jesus has come from God. But their faith is still weak. They do not realize their need for God to enlighten them with his Spirit of Truth. Jesus limits what he shares with his disciples, using figures of speech, because he knows they cannot bear to hear everything he wants to tell them. He tells them that his Father is always with him; that he and his Father are one. He promises them the gifts of understanding, joy, and peace, but in the future. Because their faith is not yet deeply rooted in him, Jesus knows they cannot comprehend the reality of his coming sufferings. Nor can they conceive of how they will desert him. When Jesus tells them of his departure, his disillusioned disciples think he is promising them something right now. Sadly, Jesus predicts they will scatter and leave him alone.

On the brink of his passion and death, Jesus warns his disciples that they will face troubles in the world. But he offers himself as the key for living in peace. Their faith in him will become unshakable only when Jesus sends the Spirit of Truth upon them. Then their faith will be based upon God's love and mercy for them, rather than on their own natural abilities. The last words of his discourse seem to continue what he said at its beginning: "Do not let your hearts be troubled" (Jn 14:1), even though "in the world you will have trouble." Jesus says that if we have faith in him, we will have peace in him.

Oratio

What a consolation it is, Jesus, that you have conquered the world and you offer yourself as my peace! But how is it possible for you to conquer *my* world of daily living so that I may live in your peace? When my life is seemingly "peaceful," with no apparent difficulties, it is usually easy for me to say I believe in you. But when I face sufferings that I find hard to endure, my life becomes unbearable. Jesus, help me to place all my faith in you. Help me to see such occasions of suffering as you view them. May nothing shake my faith in you, so that I may always find my peace in you.

Contemplatio

"Have peace in me."

Tuesday of the Seventh Week of Easter

∴· · · · · · · · · · · ·∴

Lectio

John 17:1–11a

Meditatio

> *". . . everything. . . is from you."*

It's striking just how aware Jesus is that everything he has is from his Father: his authority, his disciples, his work and mission, his very words. All is from the Father, and Jesus has received all for a particular purpose: to glorify the Father. It almost seems that Jesus is obsessed with the reality that there is nothing that he hasn't received from his Father, and he glories in that truth. It is something he is proud of.

What an intimate relationship Jesus has with the Father! Everything that belongs to the Father belongs to the Son. Jesus doesn't cling to anything. Rather, he is totally at the disposition of the Father, and everything he has received is placed at the service of the Father.

This kind of utter dependency on the Father for everything sharply contrasts with the value our society places on self-sufficiency. It promotes the idea that we can do anything and get anything if we put our minds to it. Yes, the human person possesses a wealth of capacities and potentials of all kinds. But who implanted those capacities and potentials within us? Who gives fruitfulness to the work that we do and the efforts that we make? Behind everything is the faithful presence of our loving Father.

Once we recognize that the Father has given us everything, the focus of our lives changes. We begin to marvel and live in awe of a God who desires to be so involved in our lives that he shares from his fullness to fill our poverty. The more we acknowledge him as the Giver of all we are, the less we need to hoard, to cling, to defend, or to fight for what we have. Ultimately nothing is ours, and yet everything is ours.

Oratio

Jesus, you are the Master of Gratitude. Your words, your example, your life reveal a continual awareness of the Father's love flowing through you, and of his gifts being showered upon you. Help me to model my life upon yours. May gratitude mark my life also. May giving thanks become a way of life so that I may continually glorify you and help others to do the same.

Contemplatio

Father, all I am and all I have is from you.

Wednesday of the Seventh Week of Easter

❖ · · · · · · · · · · · · ❖

Lectio

John 17:11b–19

Meditatio

> *". . . so that they may share my joy completely."*

Sharing his joy with us is important to Jesus. In this earnest petition to his Father, Jesus prays that his disciples share his joy. He wants *us* to share his joy. So, what is the joy of Jesus? What does he mean by "share my joy completely"?

We experience one kind of joy from things such as beautiful objects, lovely weather, good food, and so forth. These things are a source of delight and pleasure for us; they are gifts of God, and he is delighted that we find joy in them. Like us, Jesus knew these joys in his life. He found joy in sailing across the Sea of Galilee, in eating with his friends, in seeing fields of grain and meadows of flowers. But when he prays for us to share his joy completely, Jesus is not talking about these kinds of joy.

He is speaking about a deeper, more complete joy. Psalm 4, a prayer of trust in God during tribulation, says, "But you have given my heart more joy than they have when grain and wine abound" (v. 8). This is a profound joy that comes from communion with God deep within, even in the midst of trouble or in the absence of material joys.

This is the joy that Jesus has and wants to share with us. The joy of Jesus comes from his relationship with the Father in the Holy Spirit. His participation in the communion of love in the Trinity brings the joy of loving and of being loved. A bottomless well of this deep joy overflows in Jesus' heart. No suffering can overcome it. It drowns out all pain and sorrow. It lasts forever.

This is the joy he wants us to share completely.

Oratio

Jesus, I thank you for this glimpse into the deep, inexhaustible well of joy that flows from within you. I want to share it completely. Give me this deep joy of loving and being loved, to experience more deeply the communion of love with you that I've had from my baptism. I am amazed to hear you speak of this joy in the face of your passion. I ask you to touch me with it, in times of suffering, when I need reminding.

Contemplatio

You are the God of my joy.

Thursday of the Seventh Week of Easter

:·············:

Lectio

John 17:20–26

Meditatio

> *". . . as you, Father, are in me and I in you,*
> *that they also may be in us. . . ."*

Today's text is the final segment of the prayer of Jesus at the Last Supper. Previously he prayed for grace and strength for his disciples. Now he looks ahead in time to all those who will come to know him through their witness. We stand in the ranks of those who have heard and come to believe "through their word."

As we listen to this heartfelt conversation, we can only feel that Jesus is giving us a glimpse of his loving relationship with the Father. For his followers, Jesus asks the gift of unity. And this prayer bore copious fruits among the early Christians, who were known by their love for one another. It was a common practice for those of greater means to willingly place their material goods at the service of all those in need.

But Jesus is not content with asking only for unity and harmony in the community of believers. He wants even more wondrously to draw us right into the union he shares with the Father. ". . . I in them and you in me, that they may be brought to perfection as one." Here we stand in the realm of mystery. Jesus' heart is overwhelmingly full as he completes his earthly mission.

As he prepares to return to the Father, it is as if he cannot bear to be separated from us. "Father, they are your gift to me. I wish that where I am they also may be with me."

Earlier, in chapter 15, Jesus speaks of remaining in him, or of *abiding*. This seems to be both an invitation and a gift. Here again, Jesus seems to reveal his hunger for intimacy with us. This even includes a *mutual* indwelling and opens up for us a true participation in his own union with the Father. After the resurrection Jesus promises the gift of the Spirit, that marvelous outpouring of the love of the Father and the Son.

Oratio

Thank you, Lord Jesus, for all those who, by their teaching and example, have shared their faith and have helped me to come to know you. Grant that all Christians might be drawn closer to the unity you desire for us, so that together we might become a radiant witness to a world searching for Truth.

Help me to open my heart in loving receptivity to your amazing gift of the divine indwelling. I welcome you into my inner sanctuary and give you loving adoration, praise, and worship. May your divine Presence in my soul make me always more fruitful in love for the life of the world.

Contemplatio

Jesus, I want to be *with you*, where you are. Help me now to *remain in you*.

Friday of the Seventh Week of Easter

:·············:

Lectio

John 21:15–19

Meditatio

> *"Lord, you know everything; you know that I love you."*

Long before Peter was crucified for his fidelity to the Lord, Jesus asked him three times, "Simon, son of John, do you love me more than these?" Peter's heartfelt response echoes the response of countless disciples, saints, and martyrs from every culture and epoch of Christianity's long history. It is love and love alone that gives value to the gift of our life to God and to our acceptance of his will.

How many times we must stretch forth our hands in surrender! The martyrs faced fear, misunderstanding, and pain as they handed over their lives as faithful witnesses to Jesus. While we may not be called to that kind of radical witness, many times we need to accept realities, people, and events that we naturally resist and cannot change. Marriage and the birth of a child are strong moments when a young couple take a leap of faith. Ordination and the profession of religious vows are intense occasions when lives are given over in complete surrender. As we age, we often have to endure sickness, diminishing strength, and dependence on others. The acceptance of the daily burdens of life and fidelity to our primary commitments are all ways that we are called to grow in prayer and trust.

We may often feel fearful to take a risk of faith. We are afraid that God will ask too much and that we will fall short. God understands this fear! Yet, whatever happens, God is with us and invites us to follow him. Sad and painful events will happen in our lives, but we have no reason to be afraid, because we are never alone. The phrase "Do not be afraid!" occurs many times in Scripture because God wants to assure us of his presence at all times.

Oratio

Jesus, Good Shepherd, you first stretched forth your hands for me and showed your love to the end. May I pour out my life for love of you and your people. May I not run away from my Christian vocation when I feel afraid of witnessing to you before others. Help me to be faithful until I enjoy the fullness of your presence. May your Spirit's gift of fortitude strengthen me to proclaim the truth in love, so that your word may find a home in the hearts of all with whom I live and work.

Contemplatio

Jesus, you are my way; help me to follow you.

Saturday of the Seventh Week of Easter

❖ ⋯⋯⋯⋯ ❖

Lectio

John 21:20–25

Meditatio

> *"You follow me."*

Today's Gospel passage allows us to enter into the heart of Peter. Throughout his journey with Jesus, Peter has grown in a deeper union with him. Yet he still has something to learn, as we see from the way Jesus gently scolds Peter in response to his question. This is certainly encouraging for us, who are also journeying with Jesus. We are not the only ones who need to grow in our understanding of discipleship.

In the passage right before this, Jesus tells Peter, by way of an image, that he will experience suffering and death. So, pointing to the beloved disciple, Peter asks Jesus, "What about him?" Jesus responds by saying, "What concern is it of yours? You follow me." Jesus is telling Peter to mind his own business and keep his eyes on Jesus, not on what others are doing or not doing.

We can take Jesus' response to Peter as an invitation to keep the eyes of our mind and heart on Jesus, focusing on him and not on things that worry or discourage us. We are not to fret over God's will for other people, nor to anxiously compare ourselves with others. Certainly we bring others to Jesus in prayer, but in such a way that we are focused on Jesus, not on those for whom we are praying.

Jesus' response is also an invitation to grow in deeper intimacy with him. Our times of prayer are meant to be encounters with Jesus, and him alone. It is only with a single-minded attention on Christ that we can let go of our fears. As we come to realize that *it is not we who live, but Christ who lives in us*, we can slowly allow our anxieties and worries about comparing ourselves with others melt away. We begin to experience the freedom of being children of God.

Oratio

Jesus, help me to grow in a deeper understanding of your love for me. May your love soak up all my fears and anxieties. May your love dwelling in me transform my energies and root my choices. Look with love on those persons about whom I especially care. *(Pause and call them to mind.)* I bring them all to you and entrust them to your love.

Contemplatio

Fix your eyes on Jesus.

Pentecost—
Years A, B, and C

∵ · · · · · · · · · · · · ∵

Lectio

John 20:19–23

Meditatio

"When the doors were locked. . . ."

Today we celebrate Pentecost, and the Church asks us this great question: Is your heart open to the Holy Spirit? He has been sent to us through the door of salvation opened by the death and resurrection of Christ. Yet, like the apostles and disciples who had witnessed the marvels of the life, teaching, suffering, and death of the Lord, and then the glorious, astounding events of his life resurrected, we may have closed and locked our door.

Why? It isn't that we don't believe all that Christ taught, or what we have experienced of the power of his grace in the sacraments and in our daily lives. It is perhaps that our faith has been stunned by the realization of what has taken place. Salvation is more than we hoped for, we who live our days in this world.

We often plod along from day to day hoping for the best. We may only have a vague idea of what that best might be. Our daily concerns and cares may cloud our vision of faith.

And so, we may be hiding in fear of the stunning act of love we have just lived in the Lent and Easter seasons. Fear is the natural reaction. We fear our very fearfulness.

Today we open the doors of our hearts and let in hope and healing, like the sun's rays coming through the clouds. Today the Holy Advocate comes to fill us with wisdom, fortitude, and zeal. The Spirit brings all these things to our minds. He strengthens our resolve to live as true followers of Christ, and he fills our heart with fire.

Oratio

Lord, you stand at the door of my heart and knock. Sometimes I keep you waiting. I hesitate to open my door. I am unsure of your request. Other times I am distracted. Let me just finish with what I am doing before I let you come in. Why do I wait? Why do I fear your visit? Come to me with the fire of your love. Fill me with wisdom; fortify my spirit; make me zealous for your reign. Send your Spirit. Come to me, Lord, you are always welcome!

Contemplatio

"He breathed on them and said: 'Receive the Holy Spirit.'"

List of Contributors

:·············:

Celebrate the Church's great seasons of grace by praying *lectio divina* with the Daughters of St. Paul.

ADVENT GRACE
Daily Gospel Reflections
By the Daughters of St. Paul
0-8198-0787-7
$7.95

LENTEN GRACE
Daily Gospel Reflections
By the Daughters of St. Paul
0-8198-4525-6
$7.95

Continue to celebrate the grace of God in everyday life through *lectio divina* with the Daughters of St. Paul.

ORDINARY GRACE
WEEKS 1 – 17
Daily Gospel Reflections
By the Daughters of St. Paul
0-8198-5442-5
$9.95

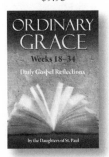

ORDINARY GRACE
WEEKS 18 – 34
Daily Gospel Reflections
By the Daughters of St. Paul
0-8198-5443-3
$9.95

BOOKS & MEDIA

A mission of the Daughters of St. Paul

As apostles of Jesus Christ, evangelizing today's world:

We are CALLED to holiness
by God's living Word and Eucharist.

We COMMUNICATE the Gospel message
through our lives and through all
available forms of media.

We SERVE the Church
by responding to the hopes and needs
of all people with the Word of God,
in the spirit of St. Paul.

For more information visit our website:
www.pauline.org.

BOOKS & MEDIA

The Daughters of St. Paul operate book and media centers at the following addresses. Visit, call or write the one nearest you today, or find us on the World Wide Web, www.pauline.org

CALIFORNIA

3908 Sepulveda Blvd, Culver City, CA 90230	310-397-8676
2650 Broadway Street, Redwood City, CA 94063	650-369-4230
5945 Balboa Avenue, San Diego, CA 92111	858-565-9181

FLORIDA

145 S.W. 107th Avenue, Miami, FL 33174	305-559-6715

HAWAII

1143 Bishop Street, Honolulu,HI 96813	808-521-2731
Neighbor Islands call:	866-521-2731

ILLINOIS

172 North Michigan Avenue, Chicago, IL 60601	312-346-4228

LOUISIANA

4403 Veterans Memorial Blvd, Metairie, LA 70006	504-887-7631

MASSACHUSETTS

885 Providence Hwy, Dedham, MA 02026	781-326-5385

MISSOURI

9804 Watson Road, St. Louis, MO 63126	314-965-3512

NEW YORK

150 East 52nd Street, New York, NY 10022	212-754-1110

PENNSYLVANIA

Philadelphia—relocating	215-676-9494

SOUTH CAROLINA

243 King Street, Charleston,SC 29401	843-577-0175

VIRGINIA

1025 King Street, Alexandria, VA 22314	703-549-3806

CANADA

3022 Dufferin Street, Toronto, ON M6B 3T5	416-781-9131

¡También somos su fuente para libros, videos
y música en español!